CHOOSE A SIDE

Choose a Side

A Beyond the Field Blueprint for Baseball Success

Erik Wagle

©2025 All Rights Reserved. No portion of this book may be reproduced, stored in a retrieval system, or transmitted in any form or by any means—electronic, mechanical, photocopy, recording, scanning, or other—except for brief quotations in critical reviews or articles without the prior permission of the author.

Published by Game Changer Publishing

Paperback ISBN: 978-1-966659-12-9

Hardcover ISBN: 978-1-966659-13-6

Digital ISBN: 978-1-966659-14-3

www.GameChangerPublishing.com

DEDICATION

This book is dedicated to all of my current and former players who have helped shape me and the career path that led to this book. Your loyalty, belief, and ability to think differently have inspired me to continue to break through with this message.

I would also like to dedicate this book to everyone who has mentored me throughout my career. My former coaches were the ones who constantly showed me the incredible impact that coaches can have on the lives of their athletes, and that inspired me to go in this direction with my career. A special dedication goes to the mentors I had throughout my journey as a player and young coach, including Mark Cummins at Live Oak High School, Doug Robb at San Jose City College, John Goelz at Sonoma State University, and Walt White at Cal State Monterey Bay. You did not know it at the time, but you were teaching me how to lead with a players-first mindset and how to build this thing the right way with the right moral compass.

And finally, this book is dedicated to my family. My journey has not been standard, and you have allowed me to forge my own path and explore this world through my own lens. Your patience and acceptance of my approach to navigating this world have allowed me to find this place in my career and life.

READ THIS FIRST

Thank you for Choosing a Side and seeking out a better way to drive young ball players to the highest levels of the game. Please enjoy this gift from me: free access to a recruiting webinar where I can dive deep into the process of navigating the recruiting process.

CHOOSE A SIDE
A BEYOND THE FIELD BLUEPRINT FOR BASEBALL SUCCESS

ERIK WAGLE

TESTIMONIALS

"Erik Wagle has established himself as one of the premier developers of high school baseball talent on the West Coast. He connects the dots at an extremely high level for young, talented players on and off the field. He has made an incredible impact on many of my professional and amateur clients."

— Adam Karon: President and lead agent - Apex Baseball

"Erik has become one of the most innovative and outstanding people at the forefront of player development in the country. The young men he trains and mentors are, without a doubt, equipped for what they will be up against at the next levels of their careers."

— Matt Hobbs: University of Arkansas Pitching Coach/ 2024 D1Baseball Assistant Coach of the Year

"I have relied heavily on Erik's guidance to establish our training programs at Cal. His experience and comprehensive knowledge have provided the framework for our individualized player development programming. He is one of the best resources in the country when it comes to player development, health, assessment, and translating training directly to performance in games."

— Mike Neu: University of California Berkeley Head Coach/ Former Major League Baseball Pitcher

CONTENTS

Introduction	xi

PART ONE
EARLY HIGH SCHOOL PHASE

1. Fierce Focus on Developing Physically	3
2. Stay Away from Showcases and Evaluated Events	15
3. Balance in the Playing Schedule	21
4. Getting Academics in Order	31

PART TWO
PRE-RECRUITING PHASE

5. Understanding How the Recruiting Process Works	39
6. Close the Gap Physically: How to Look Like a College Player	45
7. Getting Exposure the Right Way	51

PART THREE
RECRUITING PHASE

8. Recruiting Nuts and Bolts Information	59
9. A Guide to the Recruitment Process	65
10. Making a Decision	81
11. Physical Development, Balance, and Training	91

PART FOUR
POST-COMMITMENT PHASE

12. The Time Between the Commitment and Getting to Campus	99
13. How to Keep Your Commitment	107
14. What to Expect at the College Level	113
15. What to Expect at the Professional Level	119
Conclusion	127

INTRODUCTION

This book is intended for all baseball players and families who aspire to play at the highest levels. In this book, I show players and families that there is a better way to help young baseball players reach their goals than the conventional methods typically employed. Too often, players and families focus on the wrong priorities, like exposure, travel, and field performance, instead of focusing on physical development, scalable skills, and targeted logical events.

I want to guide families and athletes away from the pitfalls and bad actors in the industry, helping them navigate the path to college and professional levels in the right way. Some of these pitfalls include attending ineffective showcases or exposure tournaments, over-investing in travel instead of training, and prioritizing skill work over physical development.

Readers will gain a holistic approach to advancing in the right way. This book will show them how to connect the dots and avoid a fragmented approach. My hope is that, after reading this book, they will have a solid understanding of what it takes to reach the highest levels of the game, navigate the process effectively, and avoid common industry pitfalls. This is a guidebook that shows them the optimal path to achieving those goals.

I am confident in my advice because I've created one of the nation's most unique baseball development ecosystems. My network includes travel organizations, high-performance facilities, and high school players, and I've linked these entities to create a system that centers on the athlete and reduces unnecessary barriers in the process. This book will help players and families avoid shortcuts, allocate resources effectively, set realistic goals, and gain a broad understanding of the high school baseball industry.

I am an entrepreneur who owns multiple businesses in the baseball development world. I'm the CEO and co-founder of the Kinetic Performance Institute in Morgan Hill, California. I'm also a co-founder and partner of Alpha Baseball, one of the nation's elite travel baseball organizations, and the head baseball coach at Saint Francis High School, one of the premier high schools in Northern California. In addition, I advise many of the top high school baseball prospects in Northern California and around the nation.

I grew up in Morgan Hill, a small town on the southern edge of the Bay Area and Silicon Valley. I led a mostly typical life in a sports-oriented family. My journey through college baseball was fairly standard, but I was deeply influenced by exceptional coaches and mentors who helped shape my philosophy. Their guidance and support were instrumental in steering me toward professional coaching and have profoundly shaped my approach to developing athletes to reach the highest levels of the game.

My foundational principle is centered around the players I coach and guide. I strive to put them at the heart of the process, ensuring

INTRODUCTION

all their needs are met with care and logic. Supporting their growth has been the cornerstone of the success I've achieved in my career.

How did I reach this point? A strong work ethic has driven much of my success—a value instilled in me from a young age by my family. From early on, my priority was always to outwork everyone else. While there are many reasons for my achievements, sheer dedication and hard work have been key. Another essential factor has been a relentless focus on always doing what's best for the player. This commitment has fostered a player-centered approach across my training, travel, and high school programs, empowering athletes to lead the process and invest fully in it. Witnessing their accomplishments has been the most rewarding aspect of my life.

This has been my guiding principle: From my early days as a coach to my recent business successes, I have always prioritized what's best for the athlete and allowed everything else to fall into place.

I am eager for players and families to embark on this journey with this new approach and perspective. Dedicating themselves to navigating this process with logic and clarity will unlock potential and insight that may have been inaccessible otherwise.

PART ONE

EARLY HIGH SCHOOL PHASE

CHAPTER 1

FIERCE FOCUS ON DEVELOPING PHYSICALLY

The early days of high school should be intensely focused on building physical strength and increasing body weight. The physical foundation developed at this stage will provide the player with essential building blocks to support their performance and development throughout their journey. Unfortunately, too many athletes spend too much time playing games and working on "small" skills rather than building the "big" physical skills that scale to the highest levels of the game. Finding a facility like KPI can be essential at this age, as it's typically when most athletes begin to differentiate their approach and take the right path.

GAINING WEIGHT: THE DO'S AND DON'TS

Gaining weight is key to physical development, especially for young athletes in early high school. Increased body weight strongly correlates with high performance and on-field production. Generally, the bigger and stronger players tend to be the best at most levels. By increasing body weight, players are able to produce more force and enhance all their skills.

One of the primary methods to gain weight is to win the calorie game—you need to consume more calories than you burn. Most young athletes are naturally lean and burn calories efficiently. Thus, athletes need to focus on turning the equation in their favor. Some main strategies include eating large meals for breakfast, lunch, and dinner, with protein as a primary focus. Breakfast is especially critical, as athletes haven't consumed calories for about eight to ten hours, so a high-calorie start helps set a solid foundation for the day, along with lunch and dinner.

These main meals can be a challenge during the school day, as classes often prevent consistent calorie intake. Many athletes rely on either a light-packed lunch or a school-provided meal, which is often insufficient. We recommend athletes pack snacks to fill these gaps between meals. Protein bars, trail mix, pre-made protein shakes, and other high-calorie, high-protein snacks are ideal between meals.

This strategy also helps them keep up with their caloric needs, as young athletes often burn through their calories in just two or three hours. Even a 1,000-calorie breakfast can be used up quickly, after which the metabolic process begins to search for more energy elsewhere, often drawing from fat. Since young athletes generally have low body fat, the body may start pulling from muscle stores, which we want to avoid. Muscles should store energy, not give it away. Eating a 500–600 calorie snack between meals is therefore crucial.

Lunch is another big factor. We want athletes to either pack a high-quality lunch or rely on a nutritious school option. Similarly, the goal should be around 1,000 calories with a focus on high-protein, whole foods. The afternoon is critical because athletes reading this book are likely going to train or practice after school. If they eat lunch around 12 or 12:30, attend two afternoon classes, then train or practice, they might not eat again until 7:30 or 8 p.m.—an eight-hour gap. During this time, they've likely burned a lot of calories, so it's vital they consume plenty of calories before their training session.

Once again, trail mix, pre-made protein shakes, and protein bars are useful options, providing another 500–600 calories, followed by a 1,000-calorie dinner. Particularly dedicated athletes could consider having a small meal before bed. For the truly committed, waking up in the middle of the night to have a peanut butter and jelly sandwich or a glass of milk can help to further expand the daily calorie intake needed for optimal development.

The following provides an example of a sample meal plan a high school student can follow to gain weight:

KINETIC PERFORMANCE INSTITUTE

Meal Plan Template (Sample)

A well-balanced nutritional plan is the key to any training program. Proper nutrition ensures that the body is able to gain lean muscle mass, recover quickly, create sustainable energy, and have a proper metabolic function. While training, you should ingest at least 1 gram of protein per pound of body weight a day. This will ensure that your muscles are getting the proper fuel to build lean mass and recover quickly. To ingest that amount of protein, lean meats need to be added to every meal, and two protein shakes a day should be consumed.

The following should be included in every meal:

- Protein - All meat, fish, peanut butter, protein powder/drinks, beans, dairy, nuts
- Fiber - Fruits, vegetables, beans, oatmeal, whole wheat products, nuts
- Complex Carbs - Whole wheat bread/pasta/cereal/grains, oatmeal, nuts
- Simple Carbs - Fruits (variety of colors), vegetables (variety of colors), juices (100%)
- Dairy Products - Milk, yogurt, cheese

All diet types should be eating five meals a day every 2–3 hours. This ensures that your metabolism stays active, your energy stays consistent, and your lean muscle production is always happening. **Fast food should be avoided at all costs... it provides empty calories, and the processed nature of the food can seriously compromise any potential gains!**

Bulk Up Plan: 4,000-6,000 calories a day (adjust calories to need)

CHOOSE A SIDE

Breakfast (1000+ calories)

- Complex Carbs/Fiber - Whole wheat cereal/bagel/toast, oatmeal
- Protein - Bacon, ham, peanut butter, lunch meat, protein powder in oatmeal/cereal
- Simple Carbs - Banana, apple, juice (100%)
- Dairy - Milk, yogurt

Snack #1 (500-800 calories) - Protein Shake, nuts, dried fruit, PBJ, Powerbar

- Lunch (1000+ calories)
- Complex Carbs/Fiber - Whole wheat sandwich, beans, nuts
- Protein - Lunch meat, chicken breast, peanut butter
- Simple Carbs - Apple, orange, melons, pears, carrots, cucumber, etc.
- Dairy - Milk, yogurt, cheese on sandwich

Snack #2 (500-800 calories) - Protein Shake, nuts, dried fruit, PBJ, Powerbar

- Dinner (1000+ calories)
- Complex Carbs/Fiber - Whole wheat pasta, brown rice
- Protein - Steak, Chicken, pork chops, beans
- Simple Carbs - Fruit, cooked vegetables, edamame
- Dairy Cheese, milk, yogurt (dessert)

DON'TS FOR GAINING WEIGHT

First, avoid eating a lot of empty calories. Many of the empty calories we consume come from highly processed foods like fast food, candy, sodas, and chips. While these foods contain calories, they lack nutritional value and won't help gain and store the right kind of energy. Even if you gain calories from them, it's not the type of calories that leads to lean muscle mass, which is the goal. So, definitely avoid highly processed foods and empty calories.

Another point is not to focus solely on the big meals. Many athletes get stuck on just eating breakfast, lunch, and dinner, but the gaps between these meals can lead to calorie deficits that can be detrimental to the weight-gaining process.

Another *don't* is consuming a lot of fast food. While this overlaps with the issue of empty calories, fast food generally doesn't support lean muscle mass or provide good calories. Instead of opting for big-chain fast food, consider places like Chipotle, a taqueria, or a local deli. These alternatives often have more nourishing food with better protein sources than the processed options from major fast food chains.

NUTRITION AND SUPPLEMENTS

For nutrition, building a solid foundation of high-protein, whole carbohydrates—like rice and similar foods—is essential. Ideal protein sources are typically animal-based, with a preference for grass-fed beef and organic chicken, which contain fewer preservatives and chemicals. Other good protein options include high-calorie protein powders, particularly whey protein, from quality sources without fillers or preservatives. Additionally, many premade protein shakes are effective sources of protein.

Athletes should also include both complex and simple carbohydrates. Examples of complex carbohydrates are rice and potatoes, which are whole foods without processing. Bread can be an option, but since it's processed, it may lack the nutritional value that benefits athletes. Simple carbohydrates, like fruits and vegetables, are also essential for a well-rounded nutritional intake.

There are also supplements that can help meet an athlete's needs for fruits, vegetables, and vitamins, either through a multivitamin or powders that can be added to smoothies and shakes. Creatine is another excellent, safe supplement for weight gain. It is a naturally occurring substance in the body and has been extensively researched. Families should look for high-quality creatine powder without fillers that are NCAA-approved.

BUILDING HORSEPOWER: FORCE DEVELOPMENT

Force development is different from strength. While strength is the ability to lift weights, force is the ability to apply that strength during athletic movements. For baseball players, force development is critical. They need to produce a lot of force from the ground—known as ground reaction force—and use it efficiently and quickly. Every movement in baseball involves generating force from the ground, having it returned to the player rapidly, and transferring it through the kinetic chain (lower body > rotation > upper body).

That's why it's essential for baseball players to engage in baseball-specific training styles that focus on force production. This attribute often determines an athlete's success at higher levels of baseball. It's rarely about skill alone; rather, it's often that they lack the necessary force production. This force can be measured by tools like force plates, which we use at KPI to measure the braking rate of force development—the ability to generate force when decelerating and jumping. This force usually originates from the anterior chain, the muscles in the front of the body that drive into the ground. Exercises like jumping and squatting can help develop the type of force needed, and young athletes should focus on these movements as they apply to all areas of baseball. Athletes should concentrate on large movements and driving into the ground to improve force production.

Generally, about 70 to 80 percent of our high school athletes need force development, which is why we emphasize it strongly in the younger ages. We incorporate a lot of squatting patterns and jumping exercises to stimulate the central nervous system. This involves removing the elastic energy from their jumps and having them jump from a standstill, such as a seated position, or simply jumping as high as possible from a standing position. These techniques are very effective at training the central nervous system to produce more force.

For hitters, using the ground to generate force and transfer energy is a crucial skill. It allows them to push off their back foot, transferring energy through the kinetic chain and out through their swing. Similarly, pitchers use one leg to generate force into the ground, propelling them down the mound toward their target, ideally with high velocity. Even on defense, movements like catching the ball, gathering on the back leg, and throwing involve force production that is similar to both pitching and hitting.

Another important factor is running speed, which is often misunderstood. Many think quick toe-tapping movements develop speed, but speed is actually a result of force production. The foot flattens, generating force into the ground, and running fast simply depends on how quickly you can return that force and push it into the next step. The ability to generate force, jump high, and run fast are essential attributes for a successful baseball player.

USE OF TECHNOLOGY TO GUIDE PHYSICAL DEVELOPMENT

As athletes enter high school and begin focusing on physical development to assess if they're capable of playing at the college level, technology can provide valuable insights. It can reveal exactly where an athlete currently stands, what they need to work on, and how far they are from meeting important metrics for higher levels of the game, such as throwing velocity, swing speed, and running speed.

At KPI, we use advanced technology to measure and evaluate our athletes' performance. We can assess their standing to a high degree of accuracy using methods such as force plates to measure force, laser timers for running speed, bat sensors for bat speed, and radar guns and ball monitors for throwing velocity. For younger athletes just entering high school, these tools are crucial for determining if they're ready to be evaluated in a showcase setting. If an athlete falls short in these metrics and isn't at a college level, there's no reason for them to be evaluated by college or professional scouts, as they don't yet measure up physically.

These metrics provide a highly accurate evaluation of an athlete's current status and offer objective data on areas needing improvement. This information enables them to train more effectively, dedicating their time, money, and energy—finite resources—to targeted training rather than engaging in general training or, even worse, attending multiple showcases with the assumption that schools or colleges might be interested. In reality, these institutions may have little interest if the athlete doesn't meet their force development standards.

At KPI, in addition to the methods and metrics discussed above, we also maintain normative data on the performance metrics of higher-level players who train with us, as well as Division I and professional benchmarks. This allows us to evaluate the current standing of younger athletes and provide clear guidance on where they need to focus to achieve their goals.

OBJECTIVE VERSUS SUBJECTIVE PROCESS

The traditional process for progressing from high school to the college level is often highly subjective. Typically, a coach positions themselves as an authority in the athlete's development, with the athlete relying on the coach's opinions regarding areas for improvement, the steps needed to progress, and what they should focus on to reach the next level. We find this approach to be unsound for skill development necessary for recruitment and advancement because it relies heavily on subjective judgment. At KPI, we use the data from our normative dataset to create an objective developmental process, allowing athletes to understand exactly where they are deficient and what specific actions they need to take to reach their goals. This objective approach is far more effective than relying solely on a coach's opinion. After all, what if the coach is wrong? Betting your entire dream on their opinion is a risky choice.

We don't want athletes relying on someone's opinion to achieve their dreams. Using objective data is a much more efficient way to make progress and reach goals. This is why technology and data are essential for guiding decisions in training, evaluations, resource allocation, and focus areas. Depending on data rather than opinions is 100 percent the best way to navigate this process.

Skipping steps can be tempting, but the journey to building force development, lifting weights properly, and reaching recruitable levels takes time and hard work. Many kids find it uncomfortable and tedious, and lifting weights isn't always enjoyable. Parents might also feel inclined to hide their child's weaknesses, making it easy to skip this essential foundation-building phase.

What often happens instead is that people opt for showcases or evaluation tournaments, thinking they can sidestep the hard work. Unfortunately, this often results in wasted time, particularly during those early years that should be spent developing a strong physical and force production base. This foundation is what ultimately propels athletes to higher levels. Skipping these steps may seem easier or more appealing, but it isn't sustainable or effective.

The repercussions of skipping this foundational phase are significant. Athletes who avoid building a strong physical base at a young age may find themselves trying to catch up later. Physical development takes time, and if athletes don't start focusing on force development and strength during their first years of high school (or even in eighth grade), they won't have the time to develop these crucial areas later in the process. As recruiting and evaluation come around, it's challenging to play catch-up. The time and effort required for physical development can't be rushed, so skipping this step often leads to serious setbacks that are hard to overcome.

SUCCESS STORY

A recent success story of a local young man is an excellent example of doing this stage of the process right.

This young man was a late bloomer, reaching puberty later than some of the other high-level athletes training with us. He was initially skinny, not very strong, and lacked advanced skills. However, he followed our guidance without panicking and dedicated himself to physical development. Rather than attending showcases or joining exposure teams to "get seen," he focused on strength and force development over immediate skill display. Although he was tall and skinny, with low force production, he didn't rush or get discouraged. Instead, he spent the first two years of high school staying committed to the process, lifting weights four to five times a week, and using our technology to build up physically. Slowly but surely, he gained size, strength, and weight, and by the end of high school, he was throwing with high velocity and earned a Division I scholarship to a major university. This outcome might have seemed unlikely in his early years, but by choosing not to skip this step and dedicating himself to the right process, he achieved his goals.

CHAPTER 2

STAY AWAY FROM SHOWCASES AND EVALUATED EVENTS

In the traditional sense, showcases and exposure tournaments can provide useful value to high-level players. Showcases are individual events where a player can theoretically pay to attend with the expectation that college coaches and potentially professional scouts will be there. Exposure tournaments are similar, with the assumption that competition will be intense and college and professional scouts will attend. These events are often marketed as essential, but that couldn't be further from the truth. While a few select showcases and exposure tournaments may offer real value to the right players, these are rare, and most players are not physically capable or skilled enough to benefit from these events.

The showcase and evaluative tournament side of the industry is arguably the dark side of the industry, preying on the indecision, anxiety, and lack of knowledge in young baseball players and their families.

THE ATTENDANCE REALITY FOR COLLEGE COACHES

Firstly, these events only have value if the player is good enough to be evaluated. College coaches and professional scouts have limited time to assess all the players out there, so they avoid wasting time. They're not searching for "diamonds in the rough;" they're looking for athletes who fit their criteria for college athletics. In the early stages of high school, it's unlikely they'll attend random showcases or tournaments hoping to discover unknown talent. Metrics and technology are truly the way to first evaluate whether an athlete can perform well in these settings.

UNDERSTANDING THE REGISTRATION STANDARDS OF A SHOWCASE

One way to determine if a showcase is legitimate is by looking at its admission standards. The term "showcase" has become watered down over the years. Originally, it was an exclusive event for high-level players; now, almost any event can be labeled a showcase.

The issue here is that a showcase implies college or professional scouts will be present to evaluate players, yet most of the time, they aren't. As mentioned, colleges don't usually attend random events looking for random players; they attend higher-level events with a strong concentration of good players. So if anyone can register for the event, there are no admission standards, you don't need a recommendation from a high-level coach, or there is no screening process for the athlete; it's probably not a reputable event. It's likely just a money grab masquerading as a "showcase." College coaches and scouts attend reputable events where they know a large number of strong players will participate, and these events rarely allow open admission.

BEWARE OF MONEY GRABS

Many organizations take people's money instead of providing a true showcase that includes colleges and pro scouts. Another common occurrence, especially at lower-level events, is that showcase organizers pay college coaches to attend. Often, these coaches are lower-level assistants who don't earn as much as head coaches or primary assistants. What happens is that the organizer pays these coaches to attend and advertises their presence, but the coaches themselves may not be paying much attention and likely don't have decision-making authority in the recruiting process. Therefore, another way to evaluate the quality of an event is by considering which coaches are in attendance. If lower-level assistants are present, it's probably not a high-quality event. Reputable organizations usually run many events, so it's essential to screen these events carefully to find the worthwhile ones.

Knowing whether other skilled players are attending is also crucial, even though it can sometimes be difficult to find this information. However, the same principles apply: Avoid low-level events that lack college coverage and use these guidelines to judge whether an event is worthwhile.

Value of Investing in Training Over Exposure

There's far greater value in taking the money required to attend these events and investing it in training. Often, these events cost between $400 to $600 or even more. If the events are out of town, families have additional costs like gas, hotels, and meals, which can add up to thousands of dollars, especially when travel is involved. For younger athletes, this money is far better spent and offers a higher return on investment if it's directed toward physical development. Using that $500 for a month of training will yield much more in the long term, during the recruiting process, and in reaching college or professional levels by building a strong strength and movement foundation at this stage rather than chasing events that won't provide real value. Avoid the "exposure trap"; chasing exposure isn't the way to go.

IT'S EASY TO GET EXPOSURE

There's an old saying: If you're good enough, they will find you. While this may not be 100 percent true, it's mostly accurate. Today, getting evaluated and gaining exposure is not difficult. Every college in the nation hosts on-campus recruiting events, including college prospect camps. Any player can attend these camps and showcase their skills directly in front of college coaches. With the advent of cell phone videos and emails, players can easily send videos to any college coach in the country, allowing them to be seen. In the pre-cell phone era, exposure was a greater challenge, but that's no longer the case. Any player can gain exposure at any time. Relying solely on showcases and exposure tournaments, hoping to catch a college coach's attention, is no longer an effective strategy. It's a waste of time, money, and energy—all of which, as noted previously, are finite resources—when exposure is readily available. These days, gaining exposure is incredibly easy.

. . .

Prioritize Development Over Exposure

Focus on development; prioritize becoming good enough to be noticed. I always ask athletes, "What are you exposing? That you're 30 pounds lighter than the average college player? That you're not yet strong enough or that you don't throw or swing hard enough?" You don't want those shortcomings exposed. Wait until you're truly ready before seeking exposure. Focusing on development is essential at this stage because, when colleges evaluate athletes, they want to see players who are ready.

They're looking for athletes who physically look like college baseball players and demonstrate a high level of skill. This is why emphasizing physical development at this age is crucial.

Young athletes who train at KPI not only receive training focused on physical development but also benefit from assistance with identification, exposure, and the recruiting environment. As mentioned previously, we collect hundreds of thousands of data points to create normative data, which we share with athletes to inform their training. This allows us to show them where they are lacking and what they need to improve. We also produce high-quality videos and reports using our technology, which can be a significant advantage in the recruiting process.

CAUTIONARY TALE

An example of someone chasing exposure is a young man who has trained with us off and on through the years. He had an older sister who was a high-level athlete who advanced to the Division I level in a different sport, and his parents attempted to follow a similar path for him. His parents felt the sister could have received more opportunities if she had done more "exposure" events but misapplied that logic for his process, not realizing he was in a much different situation and that the process in baseball can be much different than other sports. Rather than focusing on his development, they took him to play for multiple travel teams and attend numerous showcases, tournaments, and college prospect camps, hoping that college coaches might take an interest in him—even though the rules prohibited colleges from speaking with him directly. They essentially wasted the first two years of his high school career by chasing exposure at these events.

When his junior year arrived—the true recruiting season—he simply wasn't big enough, strong enough, or skilled enough to be recruited. He played his junior spring season, but unfortunately, he had a poor year. The family could have used their finite resources—time, money, and energy—to develop the physical skills and tools he needed to make real progress toward his goals.

Eventually, his parents approached me, asking, "What will it take for him to get recruited?" I had to tell them that he wasn't skilled or physically strong enough because they had spent the past two-plus years chasing exposure rather than development. In the end, he did not play college baseball.

CHAPTER 3

BALANCE IN THE PLAYING SCHEDULE

Achieving a balance between playing competitively and training is essential for both the short- and long-term success of athletes early in their high school careers. Many families fall into the trap of saying "yes" to every playing opportunity instead of investing in proper training and development. This imbalance can hinder physical development and increase the risk of injury. KPI's approach helps athletes find the right balance, offering unbiased advice to guide families through this critical phase of the process.

The following provides a sample yearly schedule organized by season.

Sample Yearly Schedule

- **Spring: High School Season (February–May)**
    - Areas of Focus: Total commitment to the high school team and on-field success.
    - Keep in Mind: Strength and physical capacity can be maintained with 1–2 individualized training sessions per week.
- **Summer: Balance Between Playing and Training (June–July)**
    - Areas of Focus: With no school constraints, athletes should dedicate time to both training and playing.
    - Keep in Mind: If an athlete travels for tournaments, they should maintain their workout routine on the road.
- **August: Back to School Reset**
    - Areas of Focus: Play competitively, dedicate focus to physical recovery, increase strength training sessions, and adjust to the new school schedule.
    - Keep in Mind: The central nervous system can be stressed by big changes, so allow time for the mind and body to adjust as school resumes and the schedule changes.
- **Fall: Juggle School, Playing, and Training (September–October)**
    - Areas of Focus: Dedicate most of your time to training and starting strong academically. Select a few impactful tournaments for a game experience.
    - Keep in Mind: The fall season should be brief, around 6–8 weeks, to maintain balance and

sharpness without overloading the calendar with tournaments.
- **Winter: Prioritize Physical Development (November–January)**
    - Areas of Focus: Athletes should spend most of this time building a solid strength and body weight base for the upcoming season.
    - Keep in Mind: Without competition, athletes can handle more stress in training. KPI puts pitchers and position players through a 14-week winter program to gradually prepare for spring.

This schedule aligns with collegiate programs and helps prevent injuries. The undulations in training and playing periods allow athletes to recover from intense phases while still developing physically. Scheduled breaks from playing also help avoid mental fatigue and burnout.

A SOUND BALANCE BETWEEN COMPETITION AND TRAINING

For young high school athletes, it's essential to create a balanced calendar of competition and training over the course of a year. In warm-weather states, high school baseball usually begins in early February, marking the start of the competitive phase of the calendar.

This phase often lasts through mid- to late-May. Athletes should then take a two- to three-week break following the high school season, entering a low-stress phase. They can then play a two-month summer schedule in June and July. Depending on the athlete's level, this period shouldn't be too intense, allowing time to balance training, lifting, and playing, especially since there's no school constraint.

August should be free of competition. As school resumes, summer travel ball tournaments wind down, and athletes can use this time to decrease competitive stress and increase strength training. For athletes not playing a fall sport, playing some fall baseball in September and October is usually a good idea, particularly in warmer states. They should also train three to four days a week during this period. The winter, starting November 1, should then be dedicated to building the physical foundation that will support them through the rest of the year.

The months of November, December, and January should focus entirely on developing a strong physical base. This way, when baseball season begins again in February, athletes can maintain the strength they've built. Winter should not be a competitive period but a time for physical preparation. This type of alternation in the annual cycle of training and development aligns with a typical college baseball schedule, helping athletes adapt to the yearly rhythm of college sports and aligning with best practices to reduce injury rates.

SKILL DEVELOPMENT THROUGH PHYSICAL TRAINING

The winter months offer athletes a unique opportunity to fully invest in training, as they do not have to balance competition with their training schedules. Coupled with the extended breaks in the school calendar, winter is the perfect time of year to focus on building size and strength. Indeed, it's the only time when players are free to focus exclusively on this dimension of their development.

Alongside physical training, athletes can prioritize developing key skill tools that scale to higher levels of the game. It's often challenging to work on these skills during the rest of the year, as the body is overstressed from competition, and the playing schedule doesn't leave adequate time for training. Here are the top three skill areas young high school athletes should focus on during the winter:

- **Bat Speed:** Bat speed is highly correlated with offensive performance and advancement. An overload/underload swing training system, combined with individualized core training, can yield significant improvements in bat speed.
- **Pitching Velocity:** After a 6–8 week throwing ramp-up, pitchers can enter a velocity program mid-winter. Without the stress of in-game pitching, an individualized and science-based velocity program can help pitchers increase their velocity during the winter months.
- **Running Speed:** Running speed is a result of force application into the ground and how quickly that force returns to the athlete. Winter is ideal for focusing on power and force development, allowing athletes to shave valuable tenths off their running times, which will be tested in competitive seasons.

Athletes who play competitively for more than eight months a year are at a significantly higher risk of injury compared to those who play less. A balanced calendar helps keep athletes from playing competitively for more than eight months. As discussed above, our recommended approach involves six months of competitive play from February through July, taking August off, a short fall season of six to eight weeks in September and October, and dedicated physical development from November through January. This schedule helps reduce the risk of overuse injuries.

Numerous studies published by the American Sports Medicine Institute have shown increased injury risks for athletes who play more than eight months a year.[1] These studies also indicate that baseball players in warm-weather states, who typically play more, face higher injury risks than those in colder climates.

At KPI, we use advanced technology to monitor athletes' strength and fatigue levels throughout each season, ensuring they're physically prepared for both performance and health. Here's how each tool helps monitor readiness and stress:

- **Force Plates:** At KPI, our approach to the use of force plates differs from that of most high-performance facilities. Our analysis holistically balances various factors affecting central nervous system levels, physical stress, and timing. While most facilities monitor only peak force output, which can improve performance, our approach also considers health.
- **Arm Care Sensors:** For pitchers, we test shoulder range of motion, shoulder strength, and forearm strength at every training session. This data creates a baseline for each pitcher, which we can use to detect and address early signs of fatigue or decreased performance.

---

1. Fleisig, G. S., Weber, A., Hassell, N., & Andrews, J. R. (2009). *Prevention of elbow injuries in youth baseball pitchers*. Current sports medicine reports. https://pubmed.ncbi.nlm.nih.gov/19741352/

- **Force-Sensored Mound:** Our pitchers train on a mound embedded with force-sensor technology. This allows us to objectively assess pitching mechanics and identify areas of force and energy loss. It helps us detect if a pitcher's delivery changes due to fatigue or if they're losing ground reaction force due to physical adaptations.

Many athletes enter their high school season without the physical buildup they need because they played competitively through the winter, increasing their risk of injury. The majority of arm injuries in pitchers occur early in the spring, within the first two months of the season, due to inadequate winter preparation. This again underscores the value of our approach, which recommends that athletes use the winter to build strength rather than compete.

During summer training and travel ball, athletes can balance their schedules more easily since they don't have school. There's ample time to prioritize physical training while still playing enough games. Trouble arises when athletes are on the road too frequently, playing in numerous out-of-area tournaments, making it difficult to maintain physical development due to limited access to weight rooms.

Nutrition levels also often decline on the road, and the environment isn't ideal for development. Players in this phase should ensure they aren't traveling excessively and are mostly at home during the summer so they can train intensely. Having a fluctuating competition calendar provides necessary recovery periods and allows for an emphasis on physical development. During scheduled breaks, when competitive play is reduced, physical training should increase. This up-and-down rhythm, or fluctuation, is ideal because it gives athletes what they need to compete effectively.

With this balanced approach, athletes play enough baseball to improve but also avoid overstressing their bodies, allowing them to increase their strength. Most injuries occur when an athlete is tired, so this structure helps prevent fatigue and builds resilience, enabling athletes to endure healthier competitive phases. This fluctuation in the intensity of the competitive phases is a critical part of the schedule. A common trap young baseball players fall into is overplaying and undertraining, which increases injury risk.

Studies show that players in warmer states play more baseball than those in colder regions and, as a result, sustain injuries at a much higher rate. This is especially true for pitchers, who often don't have adequate rest, throwing at high-stress levels for extended periods. Consequently, injury rates spike after eight months of competitive play. Another drawback of overplaying without training is failing to develop skills that are essential for advancing in the game. As mentioned previously, key skills like throwing velocity, bat speed, and running speed are strongly correlated with advancement to higher levels, and these are hard to improve if a player is constantly competing.

In addition to injury risk, when the playing calendar is too intense and training is limited, players miss out on building the skills that are crucial for progressing in the sport. Playing too much is a double-edged sword for young athletes… they increase their injury risk, and they also dedicate time and resources away from physical training. So, while they gain "game experience," this is done at the sacrifice of health and physical development. Continually sacrificing healthy and physical development is not part of an effective strategy to advance to the highest levels of the game.

Additionally, burnout is a significant risk. The professionalization of youth sports has intensified the sports experience, with parents investing more resources. As a result, the pressure on young athletes has increased significantly. If athletes aren't given time to rest and distance themselves from the competitive aspects of the sport, they face a much higher risk of burnout. Without a love for the game or for training, if they feel constant fatigue or resentment, they won't invest the emotional energy or work ethic needed to reach the upper levels of the sport. KPI's engaging environment and player-centered approach can foster an athlete's love for training, encouraging them to invest in their development and advance their careers.

A good example of this approach is a young man we trained for several years. He grew up in a strongly baseball-focused region in Northern California, playing travel ball and participating in countless games. Although he was a good player with some talent, he hadn't attracted any recruiting interest by his junior year of high school. When he came to us for training, we created a more balanced calendar for him, prioritizing physical strength during the winter and August and striking a better balance between play and training in the spring and summer. The results were impressive. He gained weight, size, and strength, allowing his body to prepare adequately, and he began to excel on the field. He ultimately earned a Division I scholarship to a major university and now has a promising shot at a career as a professional baseball player.

CHAPTER 4

GETTING ACADEMICS IN ORDER

Academics can be a significant differentiator in the recruiting process, often representing the difference between an athlete reaching their dream school or not. Higher GPAs and test scores increase the number of schools that can recruit the athlete, opening up more opportunities. Academics can also serve as a tiebreaker between two players with similar skills: Colleges are more likely to choose the athlete with stronger academics, as it usually suggests a smoother admissions process and often reflects a solid work ethic. In life, attending a high-ranking academic institution can lead to a degree with strong earning potential.

At KPI, we offer various programs and have coaches well-equipped to advise athletes, helping them navigate this process. We provide individualized academic plans to guide each athlete toward achieving the highest standards of success. Our team has extensive experience helping athletes through this process and supporting their academic achievements.

Academics are crucial in the development of young baseball players and in positioning them for success in the recruiting process, which is highly competitive. Strong academics significantly improve the odds of a successful outcome in the recruiting process, allowing the players with higher GPAs more opportunities and favorable opinions from college recruiters. The vast majority of high school baseball players do not advance to play at the collegiate level, so the numbers are stacked against each athlete trying to advance to the next level. Having a high GPA is often the deciding factor in whether one makes it to the collegiate level.

Beating the odds to advance to the next level often involves a filtering process based on GPA. Athletes with high GPAs can be recruited by a greater number of schools in the recruiting process, which allows them to navigate that process better because they have more options. It is a process that doesn't always deliver a lot of options because the percentages and the odds are against the athlete. GPA is able not only to open up the number of schools that recruit them but also to separate them from other athletes.

It's common for colleges to evaluate two athletes of similar skill levels and choose the one with the higher GPA, as it suggests that the athlete has a proven track record of high achievement, strong work habits, and the ability to gain academic admission that might otherwise be challenging without their athletic abilities. College admissions are highly competitive, and having a high GPA can be a crucial factor.

If an athlete can balance strong baseball skills with high academics, they may gain admission to a college they might not have otherwise, especially since athletes often face lower admission standards than the general population at many schools, particularly large Division I institutions. This opportunity to earn a degree from a high-ranking institution can have a positive impact on the rest of their lives.

We've seen numerous examples of young athletes using their baseball skills and academic success to set up promising futures. Many college and professional teams see a high GPA as a sign of a strong work ethic. The reality is that most college baseball players do not complete their collegiate careers, and the same goes for professionals.

A high GPA is also a signal of discipline. It shows that a young man can balance their schedule and that they possess the work ethic and organizational skills needed to prioritize academics. It tells evaluators that this athlete understands how to allocate their time to prioritize what's important, highlighting their maturity and dedication.

LIFE AFTER BASEBALL

Getting into a strong academic university can set up an athlete for life. As we mentioned above, athletes typically benefit from lower admission standards than non-athletes, which means a high-achieving baseball player with strong academics can often gain entry to prestigious universities they might not otherwise qualify for. Many of these top academic institutions offer degrees with higher earning potential compared to universities with less rigorous standards. As athletes enter the workforce, having a degree from a respected university can make the difference in landing a job or advancing in their field, providing a competitive edge.

How to Achieve Academic Success

Achieving academic success in high school will lay the groundwork for becoming a successful collegiate student-athlete and, later, a successful professional. High school athletes should establish a routine and develop the skills that will ensure both immediate and long-term success.

Here are some strategies to ensure success and develop strong academic habits:

- **Bucket Your Life:** Student-athletes have many demands on their time: family and friends, training, playing, and school. High-achieving players organize their schedules and prioritize different areas of focus at different times. Allocate chunks of time each day to maintain a healthy balance. When it's time to focus on academics, it needs to be the priority during that part of the day.
- **Create Effective Study Routines:** Different students learn in different ways. Identify your learning style and build effective study habits around it. Visual learners may benefit from graphics created with AI or online resources. Auditory learners might excel by listening and taking notes. Interactive learners might need to review material actively through discussions. Each player should consistently practice routines that foster success based on their individual needs.
- **Get Help:** With the rise of online learning, there are numerous options for academic support. Students shouldn't hesitate to seek help from online tutors or local resources. As students advance, subjects become more

specialized, and subject-matter experts will be available to assist with specific tutoring needs.

A perfect example of balancing academics with athletic aspirations is a young man we worked with for the last 3 years of his high school journey. He comes from a less populated area of Northern California, which generally doesn't produce high-level baseball players or students with high academic achievements. Economically, it's a fairly depressed region, and he has a minority background. Fortunately, he found us at KPI for training, and we were able to support him through our non-profit and financial aid program since his family couldn't afford our services. The young man was a strong academic student, and we encouraged him to maintain his commitment to his studies.

Through his hard work and dedication, he combined his physical development with his academic strengths, ultimately earning admission to Stanford, one of the most prestigious and selective universities in the world, with unparalleled earning potential for its graduates. His life will be forever impacted by his Stanford degree, achieved in part because of his talent for baseball. His success and commitment to Stanford exemplify the outcomes that are possible with a balanced approach to development and by prioritizing academics as a central aspect of the journey, not a secondary consideration.

PART TWO

PRE-RECRUITING PHASE

CHAPTER 5

UNDERSTANDING HOW THE RECRUITING PROCESS WORKS

The recruiting process is a progression that requires a cohesive approach, logical planning, and a clear understanding of how things actually work. Too many players and families have a skewed view of the process or attempt to skip steps, setting up inevitable failure. For athletes to reach a point where they can genuinely expect to be recruited, they must meet certain physical criteria, possess advanced skills, and have demonstrated high performance in competitive settings. Once those boxes are checked, an athlete *might* be able to expect recruitment.

KPI has a deep understanding of how the recruiting process works, including the steps and milestones that need to be met before advancing. We focus on increasing the "size of the engine" early in physical development and know how to train an athlete to accelerate their progression in terms of physical development, skill acquisition, and mental acuity.

The first step is understanding how the process actually works. There is a progression from being an unrecruited athlete to a recruitable athlete, which young families need to grasp. The initial focus should be on developing the skills that matter most. Key skills for hitters include bat speed, which correlates with the ability to impact the ball and play at higher levels. For pitchers, throwing velocity is by far the best predictor of advancement, as it has the highest correlation with moving up and is a key filter in the recruiting process.

Other skills that scale to higher levels include running speed and, for defensive players, arm strength—similar to pitching velocity. All of these tools can be developed in the weight room and training facilities.

At KPI, we leverage our technology to prioritize and emphasize these skills. While on-field skills are important, our focus is on those that most impact advancement: bat speed, pitching velocity, running speed, and throwing velocity for position players. Our technology allows us to assess, measure, track, and progress our athletes toward becoming recruitable.

As young athletes approach the recruiting process, they should keep in mind that they want to build a physique that resembles those of college players. Colleges don't want to have to project what you might look like two years in the future; the more they have to guess what a player will look like in a few years, the less confident they are. Colleges want to see athletes with visible muscle structure, especially in the shoulders and hips. When size and strength are evident, colleges can better assess how a player's performance will translate to their level.

If an athlete can build muscle and approach the body weight and size of the average college player, they will have a better chance of being recruited and will attract more interest from schools. Physical skills take years to develop—such as building force, increasing bat speed, and raising throwing velocity—so this phase should emphasize physical development. While skills like perfecting the swing path, refining defense, or improving pitching accuracy are important, they can be refined later in the process.

The hardest skills to acquire later are the big physical tools needed to advance to the next level. Colleges are increasingly looking for players who can impact their programs immediately. This has become a moving target due to changes in the recruiting landscape, including the transfer portal, new rules on letters of intent, and the ability to compensate athletes through name, image, and likeness agreements.

Athletes should focus on building these physical tools in the weight room. A structured, tech-based, individualized strength program paired with proper nutrition can help them achieve the physical stature needed to reduce the difference in appearance between themselves and older college players. While college recruiters will have access to the height and weight measurements provided by a showcase or tournament provider, those are often misleading or inaccurate. Colleges want to see the players visibly look like college players because they do not usually have tangible measurements to work off of. Partnering with a facility like KPI, which has advanced technology and expertise in building size and strength, can greatly accelerate this process for young athletes.

College baseball has trended toward older players, with transfers becoming more common. Colleges are now more interested in recruiting consistent, dependable players transferring from other schools rather than taking a chance on a 17- or 18-year-old high school senior. This shift has led to an increased emphasis on physicality: colleges want to know if a player is big enough and strong enough to play at their level.

Colleges are also looking for players with standout tools, like bat speed, throwing velocity, and overall running speed, knowing that younger high school players will be competing for roster spots against older players. They seek high-energy athletes who play hard, with intensity, and with an edge—players who approach the game the right way. Colleges value coachable athletes who listen, are open-minded, and are constantly striving to improve and advance to higher levels of the game.

The stark reality is that a 22-year-old player, even with moderate skills, is almost always more consistent and effective than an 18-year-old with similar abilities. This is why more colleges are recruiting from the transfer portal instead of taking the "riskier" option of a high school senior. Because of this, high school players must work even harder to close the perceived physical gap. When training, high school athletes should bring the intensity as if they're competing for roster spots against seasoned players in their early twenties—because, in reality, they are.

In addition to physical prowess, colleges also value the mental maturity older players often possess. Older athletes have usually experienced the transition to college, adapting to life on their own, and have developed resilience. Colleges appreciate not having to manage the common adjustments freshmen face. These older players often display a stronger work ethic, are more coachable, and are better equipped to handle the demands of college baseball. Alongside physical training, athletes and their families should focus on these social, emotional, and mental aspects of development as well.

Key timelines and dates to be aware of include new NCAA recruiting rules that prevent colleges from actively recruiting a player until August 1st, before their junior year. This means that the first two years of high school are generally a non-recruiting phase. Colleges are prohibited from discussing recruiting with an athlete during this time. The only exception is if an athlete attends a camp on the college's campus, and even then, schools are only permitted to discuss general information about the school, not recruiting specifics.

After August 1st of the athlete's junior year, colleges may begin phone communication with the athlete. Starting September 1st of their junior year, the athlete and their family can be formally invited to visit the campus for recruiting purposes. Previously, a National Letter of Intent signing day took place in November of the athlete's senior year, but this has recently been discontinued. Now, there is no national letter of intent, and no binding agreement exists between the NCAA and the athlete. Instead, schools issue financial aid agreements, which are not legally binding until the athlete arrives on campus. Therefore, there is no longer an official signing day or milestone; athletes now sign a financial aid agreement that only becomes binding upon their arrival at the school.

To close this chapter, the following provides a summary of the characteristics of an athlete who is ready to enter the recruiting process:

- **Physically**
    - Proportional height and weight
    - Noticeable muscle structure
    - Heavier than 180 lbs
- **Work Ethic**
    - Lifts weights 4–5 times per week
    - Dedicates 2–3 days per week to the field
    - Daily skill work

- - Follows a structured nutrition, meal plan, and weight-gaining program
- **Mentally**
  - Calm and mature
  - Confident
  - Independent
  - Tough and resilient

If you can develop these characteristics and demonstrate them to potential recruiters, you'll have maximized your chances. In the following chapter, we'll discuss the KPI approach to getting into the physical shape you need to be in.

CHAPTER 6

CLOSE THE GAP PHYSICALLY: HOW TO LOOK LIKE A COLLEGE PLAYER

There is no more important factor in the progression of a young baseball player than getting bigger and stronger. Historically, the recruiting process has been challenging to prepare for and navigate. Now, with competition against older, physically more mature players, gaining physical ground during high school years is more critical than ever. There's an urgency to close the gap; building strength takes time, and the longer it takes, the less opportunity there is to maximize physical potential.

Using force plates daily, KPI can monitor the force production of all athletes in-house, as well as record their weight. By combining these metrics, we give each athlete a clear view of their progress toward becoming a potential college athlete.

The weight room is a young athlete's best ally for reaching the upper levels of the game. They should spend the majority of their dedicated developmental time intelligently maximizing their physical capacity and gains, as this will make the largest difference in the progression to becoming a recruitable player. With this focus, athletes are developing the essential, scalable skills that only the weight room can provide. The weight room enhances force production, body awareness, mechanics, and resilience, helping athletes stay healthy.

Here's how the weight room contributes to each key area of development and performance:

- **Body Awareness:** Baseball players need advanced proprioception (position and movement body awareness). Strength and joint stability enable players to perform athletic movements on the field and control their bodies across various movement patterns.
- **Mechanics:** Young athletes often struggle to produce athletic movements with consistency and precision due to a lack of strength and stability to control their range of motion. Strength training helps athletes synchronize movements and develop consistent mechanics, which will make them more accurate in their execution in play.
- **Resilience:** Baseball has high injury rates across all levels. Proper strength training allows young bodies to accumulate stress safely and for soft tissue to build resilience, lowering injury risk.

Gaining size and strength through the weight room also helps athletes develop a physical stature that resembles those of college or professional players. As discussed previously, the less a college has to project about a player's future potential, the more likely they are to recruit them. When a player looks physically prepared for college-level play, a college is more inclined to offer a scholarship because they don't need to make subjective projections. College baseball has shifted toward older players, with Division I schools increasingly recruiting through the transfer portal. A 22-year-old player is physically more developed than a 17- or 18-year-old, which is why many colleges prefer transfers.

In developing a collegiate-level physique, athletes should target major muscle groups. Building a strong lower body should be foundational, with squatting and hinge movements forming the base for more advanced exercises as athletes mature. For the upper body, focusing on the four main planes of motion (vertical push/pull and horizontal push/pull) ensures balanced training of large muscle groups. Core exercises should emphasize postural stabilization and rotation, with a focus on exercises like planks and medicine ball rotations rather than crunches that compromise posture.

This underscores why young athletes must work to close the physical gap, aiming to get as close as possible to an adult, collegiate-level body. They are now competing for roster spots against older athletes, a shift from past generations when players didn't face the transfer competition they do now.

GETTING MORE GRANULAR WITH TECHNOLOGY

Technology can take an athlete's training to the next level by identifying specific weaknesses as they prepare for the recruiting process, allowing for precise targeting of interventions to achieve improvements. If an athlete lacks range of motion, has slow bat speed, or exhibits subpar fastball velocity, technology can identify these issues with accuracy, making training highly specific. When an athlete excels in three or four metrics but is lacking in one or two, this is the perfect opportunity to target and improve those areas, setting them on a clear path toward recruitment success.

The following are the four main metrics that colleges look at and the goal for each one to become a Division I player:

- Pitching Velocity: 90 mph +
- Hitting Bat Speed: 68 mph +
- Position Player Throwing Velocity:
  - Catchers: 80 mph +
  - Infielders: 88 mph+
  - Outfielders: 90 mph+
- Running: 60-yard dash: 6.8 seconds or less

Technology allows athletes to be well-prepared for college recruitment, helping to identify and address any deficiencies early on. This means that when recruiters evaluate them, athletes present a complete skill set without gaps they might have missed. Technology helps athletes understand the metrics they need to meet for college-level play, enabling them to track their progress effectively. Health and wellness should also be a priority, as an injured athlete can't be recruited.

Currently, most arm injuries and surgeries in baseball occur during high school, which can severely disrupt the recruiting process. Colleges are unlikely to recruit a player recovering from surgery. High school players must prioritize their health and align their training with their goals to avoid overuse and excessive stress. Staying healthy allows them to showcase the best version of themselves. Technology supports this by using arm care sensors to monitor the strength and range of motion of pitchers' arms, ensuring they maintain appropriate strength throughout the season.

At KPI, we frequently use force plates to monitor athletes' stress levels, not only to measure force production but also to assess whether they are overstressed or fatigued. By evaluating their central nervous system's condition, we can make better decisions to manage their health and wellness, helping them compete at their best and stay on the field.

A good example of this approach to closing the physical gap is a young man who trained with us since he was 12 years old. Early in high school, he was tall and skinny, a talented but "projectable" player—meaning there was much guessing about how he'd develop physically. Starting in his sophomore year, we focused on building his strength, placing him on a meal plan to gain weight, and maintaining a strict, year-round weightlifting schedule of 3–4 times per week, along with a carefully managed throwing program that fluctuated throughout the year.

By his junior year, he had gained 20 pounds, and as he entered the recruiting process, he looked like a college player on the mound. His performance was also at a high level due to his increased strength, which allowed him to commit to a top Division I university with strong academics. When he arrived on campus, his body weight and force production were already comparable to those of his college teammates, even as a freshman. His training had fully prepared him for the significant step up to Division I, enabling him to compete and make an immediate impact, securing substantial playing time as a freshman—a rare achievement.

CHAPTER 7

GETTING EXPOSURE THE RIGHT WAY

Getting exposure the right way means ensuring the player is good enough to be exposed before putting them out there in the evaluative environment. Families can waste valuable time, money, and energy by seeking exposure before the athlete is ready. This can lead to compounding consequences, as athletes miss out on essential development opportunities, which ultimately limits the benefits of exposure. Given the competitive odds facing every player trying to reach the collegiate level, the stakes are high, and focusing on the right priorities is critical. Exposure alone does not get an athlete recruited—being good enough does.

At KPI, we regularly consult with athletes and families on when to start the recruiting process and how to determine if they're ready for it. We offer various packages to advise and guide families in making decisions during this crucial stage. We help athletes avoid premature exposure and stay committed to the development that truly matters.

When young athletes begin seeking exposure, it's essential that they approach it correctly, as there are pitfalls to avoid. Athletes should ease into the evaluative environment, which differs significantly from a competitive one. College and professional scouts aren't always focused on pure performance outcomes; they also evaluate how a player carries themselves, the effort they put into the game, how they interact with coaches and teammates, and how they handle challenges. Body language and response to failure are key traits that college coaches observe in this setting. Athletes need to display traits of resilience and grit and show the maturity to handle adversity. College recruiters and pro scouts are not very outcome-based when they are evaluating potential prospects. One of the large things they are looking for is how the athlete handles adversity, interacts with teammates and coaches, and whether they look like a seasoned, mature prospect.

In a regular competitive setting, athletes are with their teammates and simply playing the game—a familiar experience they're often skilled at. However, being observed by someone with a clipboard who could influence their future introduces a different kind of pressure. Getting accustomed to this evaluative environment is essential because it feels very different from the typical environment that athletes grow up in. Strategies to ease into this environment, rather than jumping in too quickly, include attending local, affordable college camps. Learning to perform under pressure and maintain composure while being evaluated leads to more favorable outcomes.

Here are some tips for performing well in the evaluative environment:

- **Be Normal:** Baseball is the same game at every level. Great players mentally normalize the environment, competing as they always do, regardless of where they are.
- **Understand What Scouts Are Looking For.** Athletes often try to "be big" in these moments, which can lead to them overextending and looking out of control. Trusting their skills and staying within their capabilities is key.
- **Visualize Success.** Before and during the event, athletes should train their minds to perform by visualizing successful outcomes. They should mentally place themselves in the setting, using as many senses as possible to picture themselves executing successfully. These visualizations should always be positive.
- **Learn to Breathe Properly.** Proper breathing helps manage pressure. The body's natural "fight or flight" response leads to shallow shoulder breathing, which conserves oxygen but is counterproductive to performance. Athletes should practice deep breathing into their diaphragm to activate the parasympathetic nervous system, helping them relax and distribute oxygen to their muscles more effectively.

As previously mentioned, many colleges host prospect camps, ranging from junior colleges to Division I institutions. Most athletes will have access to colleges within their region. Attending these local camps can help young athletes acclimate to the evaluative showcase environment.

Getting used to being watched and evaluated can help an athlete adjust to the less competitive, more individual format of a showcase. Playing in higher-level tournaments with regional or national teams, rather than just local teams, can further prepare an athlete for a higher level of competition and provide experience in performing under observation.

There are usually good opportunities available for travel tournaments that provide the middle ground between high-level tournaments and local tournaments. These are good opportunities to find mid-level tournaments that enable athletes to begin to get that experience. At this stage in the process, the goal should not be exposure because they're not ready yet. The goal is just to get used to this environment. For example, it's necessary to start to get a feel for how things are different and how to perform with a different stimulus and the different environmental setup. This will be of significant help later in the process, as when you are in the true exposure environment, you will already have something of a base of knowledge there. You want to resist the exposure trap.

The following represents a logical series of steps to start to enter the evaluative environment:

- **Ensure you're good enough.** Make sure your physical attributes line up well with those at the college level.
- **Go to local college prospect camps.** These are usually affordable and won't take any travel. This will help players get used to performing in front of coaches and interacting with them.
- **Start higher-level tournaments.** Seek out some travel teams and tournaments that traditionally have colleges in attendance. The colleges there might not be targeting your player, but their presence can help the player get used to the environment.

All of this should be done in accordance with what the metrics are telling the athlete. As athletes gain more exposure, they should assess any gaps in their performance relative to their training. They should integrate feedback from the field so that weaknesses can be addressed in training. High-performance facilities like KPI can help significantly with this. Athletes should benchmark their skills and performance levels, and if they aren't meeting these milestones, they should invest more in their training.

This is often the phase where athletes feel ready to enter the recruiting arena and get noticed. They may see peers starting to attend showcases and evaluative events and feel pressured to join. However, the key is to ensure they are genuinely prepared. Too often, players and parents dive in simply because these events become more accessible at this stage, or they see others participating. However, attending before the athlete is ready wastes valuable time, energy, and money.

Another risk at this stage is overexposure to college scouts. If a college sees a player multiple times—through prospect camps, showcases, and tournaments—they may start to focus on the player's weaknesses rather than their strengths. Until an athlete is fully prepared, exposure should be limited. Overexposure can lead colleges to view the player more critically, which may work against the athlete. If a college initially finds a player interesting, seeing them too often can lead scouts to "pick apart" the player's game, highlighting negatives rather than positives. This overexposure can create a negative perception.

Social media also plays a significant role in the recruiting process today. Showcase and tournament organizers are adept at using social media to make families feel they need to attend events for exposure, even when this isn't necessary. A player's social media posts have little impact on recruiting unless the athlete is good enough. Most showcase companies will post every player who pays the fees on social media. Colleges are aware of this and often don't use these posts as reliable recruiting tools. Organizers are paid to post, and parents may assume that if their child is posted on social media, a college will see and recruit them. While this may happen occasionally, it's rare. The recruiting process is much more nuanced, and typically, social media posts alone don't lead to recruitment. Likes and tags are not indications of recruiting interest; direct contact from colleges is.

Fear of missing out (FOMO) is also prevalent at this stage. Players and families often see friends or teammates attending high-profile events, which creates a sense of panic that they're missing out if they don't attend. However, this is not how recruiting works. There is still plenty of time in the recruiting process. If the player isn't ready, attending these events won't help. Instead, time, money, and energy should be invested in training and physical development.

The metrics will tell you if you're ready. Players need to train in a facility like KPI that provides objective feedback, benchmarks to follow, and a roadmap using metrics. These metrics help players determine whether they're ready to perform—whether they can confidently say, "Yes, I'm ready because my metrics meet the standards," or recognize, "No, I'm not ready yet." This awareness allows them to stay disciplined in their training, focusing on closing any gaps over the next few months. With patience and the right perspective, players can prepare themselves for exposure events. Staying committed to the development process will yield the greatest dividends in the long run.

PART THREE
RECRUITING PHASE

CHAPTER 8

RECRUITING NUTS AND BOLTS INFORMATION

It is imperative that families understand the fundamentals of the recruiting process, as this will allow them to make sound decisions based on the facts instead of falling into the problematic approaches that many bad actors present and that do not align with the recruiting calendar and other rules. Understanding the benchmarks and milestones will assist families in navigating the rough waters of the recruiting process properly.

The recruiting process follows timelines and milestones set by the NCAA and other governing bodies. Understanding the various phases and periods within the recruiting process is crucial for athletes and their families. Key periods include the *contact period*, when colleges are allowed to contact athletes freely, including off-campus visits and on-campus visits. The *dead period* restricts schools from off-campus evaluation or recruiting, though athletes can still be brought on campus for prospect camps or visits. A *shutdown period* prohibits all contact.

Phases of the NCAA Recruiting Process

- **Contact Period:** Colleges can make in-person, off-campus recruiting contacts and evaluations.
- **Quiet Period:** Colleges can make in-person contact only on campus; off-campus contacts or evaluations are not permitted.
- **Dead Period:** Colleges cannot make in-person recruiting contacts or evaluations on or off campus nor allow official or unofficial visits.
- **Evaluation Period:** Colleges can evaluate academic and athletic qualifications at off-campus events but cannot engage in in-person, off-campus recruiting.
- **Recruiting Shutdown:** No recruiting or visits are allowed, although correspondence is permissible.

There are several points throughout the year when schools cannot have any contact or perform any recruiting or evaluation with an athlete.

Some key dates include no contact (outside of camps) before August 1st of an athlete's junior year. Starting on this date, recruiting can begin, and by September 1st, campus visits are allowed. The National Letter of Intent signing period was recently eliminated, so there is no more formal signing day in the athlete's senior year.

CHOOSE A SIDE

Important Dates in the NCAA Baseball Recruiting Calendar (Subject to Change)

- **August 1 to Mid-August:** Contact Period
- **Mid-August to Mid-September:** Quiet Period
- **Mid-September to Mid-October:** Quiet Period
- **Mid-October to End of February:** Quiet Period, except for:
  - 2nd Week of November: Dead Period
  - Thanksgiving Week: Recruiting Shutdown
  - Christmas Week: Recruiting Shutdown
  - First Weekend of January: Recruiting Shutdown
- **March 1 to End of July:** Contact Period, except for:
  - Memorial Day Week: Dead Period
  - Father's Day Weekend: Dead Period
  - 4th of July Week: Dead Period

To succeed in the recruiting process, prospective college baseball players must perform well academically. The NCAA has minimum eligibility requirements that align with graduation standards but follow a sliding scale based on GPA, credits, and class types. NCAA eligibility standards are posted on their website.

Athletes must also register with the NCAA Eligibility Center at some point, ideally before entering their junior year. This registration allows the NCAA to track athletes' academic and amateur status throughout their careers. As soon as a student starts high school, the tracking of their academics and amateurism begins. During the high school years, each semester grading period is posted and eventually will be reported to the NCAA through the eligibility center. At the conclusion of high school graduation, the athlete will report their final transcripts and any testing (SAT/ACT) scores to the Eligibility Center to determine NCAA eligibility. Upon entering an NCAA institution, the athlete's NCAA ID number continues to be used to monitor academic progress toward graduation and eligibility.

Grade point average (GPA) is generally the strongest indicator of academic success and is highly valued by most NCAA schools. Since COVID, many schools have waived the SAT/ACT requirements, though some are reintroducing standardized testing for admissions. Public universities tend to have more straightforward admission criteria, often tied directly to GPA, SAT/ACT scores, and intended major, whereas private universities allow for more subjective discretion and context in admissions decisions.

Each private school sets its own admissions rules, while public university systems often standardize their requirements across institutions. In terms of levels of play, NCAA Division I represents the highest level of amateur college baseball, with a uniform eligibility standard applied across all programs.

This includes many of the larger schools we see on TV and follow. Typically, about 2 percent of high school baseball players advance to the NCAA Division I level, so athletes must be exceptionally skilled. Division II is the next level down, often offering a blend of academics and athletics, whereas Division I is strongly focused on athletics. Division II schools may place a slightly stronger emphasis on academics. They are typically smaller schools with less budget than Division I institutions, but they still support competitive athletic programs with some athletic priority.

Division III institutions prioritize academics more than athletics, often consisting of smaller private schools. They play fewer games than Division I and Division II schools, and there is a much stronger academic focus. Athletic scholarships are not available at the Division III level; however, athletes can still receive academic scholarships and merit aid.

The NAIA (National Association of Intercollegiate Athletics) is a separate governing body outside the NCAA that also holds significance in college baseball. NAIA requirements are generally less academically stringent than the NCAA's, which allows athletes who may not meet NCAA eligibility requirements to compete. The NAIA consists of a collection of college institutions that offer athletic programs as part of its structure.

Junior college baseball is also prominent nationwide. Junior colleges are two-year institutions that typically handle the general education requirements for a bachelor's degree. Academic admission standards are usually much lower, if not nonexistent. This level can be valuable for athletes, as it is generally less competitive than four-year colleges, allowing athletes to complete many of their general education requirements early. Additionally, junior college is often more affordable or even free, making it a financially smart starting point for athletes before transferring to a four-year school.

Here's a breakdown of each level of play for college baseball and an example of an athlete who would theoretically attend each level as a student-athlete.

- Division I - The highest level of amateur athletics. This is the most intense level of competition, with a fierce focus on athletics (often over academics). The players who attend this level are often the very best players in the nation and are striving to become professionals.
- Division II - This is a blend of athletics and academics and can often serve a wide range of athletes. The

admission and eligibility standards are less stringent than Division I. The players that attend this level are generally not as talented as Division I players and/or do not meet the academic or age standards of Division I

- Division III - Strong focus on academics over athletics. Generally smaller, academic-focused institutions. Players that attend these schools are generally less talented than Division I and II institutions and are much more academically oriented.
- NAIA - Like Division II, the spectrum of players and institutions can vary widely, but this is also a general mix of academics and athletics. The admissions and eligibility standards are generally lower than NCAA institutions, so the players that attend these schools might not have been eligible at NCAA institutions.
- Junior College - These are 2-year institutions that focus on academically satisfying the General Education graduation requirements. The level of play can vary widely, but generally, it would be lower than the Division I or II NCAA levels. The players attending junior colleges can also vary widely, but generally, they are those who are not ready to play at the 4-year level yet and need more time to physically develop or get their academics in order.

CHAPTER 9

A GUIDE TO THE RECRUITMENT PROCESS

One of the first challenges of entering the recruiting process is how to know if you're actually getting recruited or not. With the increase in electronic outreach and social media, it's often difficult to determine whether communication reflects genuine recruiting interest or is simply a money grab. Obtaining reliable information on the process and having trusted advisors can make it much easier to navigate and make informed decisions. The right mindset and good decision-making are crucial at this stage.

HOW TO KNOW IF YOU'RE BEING RECRUITED

This is a tricky but essential part of the recruiting process. Colleges often reach out to potential athletes, inviting them to prospect camps that help fund coaching salaries and program budgets. However, this isn't always genuine recruiting outreach—it's often just an invitation to a paid camp. Here are some ways to distinguish between real interest and general outreach.

First, consider who is reaching out. College baseball programs often have large staffs, especially at bigger Division I schools, but most recruiting is done by full-time, paid staff—typically the head coach, recruiting coordinator, or lead assistant. If one of these individuals contacts you directly, it's likely legitimate interest. If the outreach comes from a lower-level or volunteer assistant, camp coordinator, or unpaid staff member, it's probably a general invitation to a camp rather than a genuine recruiting interest.

Another factor is the personalization of the communication. Is the letter or email addressed specifically to you, with details about your abilities and situation? Or is it a vague, templated message that looks like it's been sent to many players? Personalized messages suggest actual recruiting interest, while generic messages often signal mass outreach to fill camp spots.

Genuine Indicators of Recruiting Interest

- **Personalized Letter or Email:** The head coach or recruiting coordinator sends a letter or email with specific information about you and details on setting up a follow-up conversation.
- **Texts or Calls:** A paid coach reaches out by phone to discuss recruiting, set up calls, or arrange visits. A camp invitation alone should not be considered a recruiting message.
- **Consistency:** There is regular communication from a paid coach, showing a genuine interest in staying in touch.

- **Offer for a Visit:** If a coaching staff is willing to host a visit, they are likely serious about recruiting.

If the contact is consistent, you're likely being recruited. On the other hand, if it feels like you're not being pursued actively, you may not truly be on their radar. Coaches follow certain contact rules, but good recruiters will reach out regularly if they're genuinely interested.

Another key indicator is the offer of a visit. There are two types of visits: *official* and *unofficial*. An official visit means the school covers travel expenses for you and your family. An unofficial visit, while not paid for by the school, is still a recruiting visit and often applies to local prospects. Either type of visit indicates genuine interest, as it's rare for a school to recruit a player without offering some form of visit.

CREATING OUTREACH MATERIAL

When making outreach materials, athletes should understand that colleges receive hundreds of emails and messages daily. Crafting professional, thoughtful outreach materials is essential to stand out as a legitimate prospect and to respect the time of busy coaches who receive countless communications. Here's how to approach this the right way.

EMAILS

It's crucial to remember that college coaches may receive dozens or even hundreds of emails per day. To stand out, keep your email concise, but make sure it includes all the essential information in the first go. If the college has to reply to ask for more information, that could reduce the chances of a response. So, keep emails short, but make sure they're complete. Include contact information for the athlete and parents, along with links to video clips (links work better than attachments).

The email should also include contact details for your high school coach, travel ball coach, and trainer if you have one. Additionally, attach a copy of your transcripts so the school can review your academic standing. If you have SAT or ACT scores, include a link or attachment for those as well. Essentially, the goal is to deliver all the information they need to evaluate you quickly. Next up are calls or texts. Here, it's even more important to keep things brief and respectful.

If you happen to get the cell phone number of a college coach, always respect their time. Avoid spamming them or overloading them with information. Make sure messages are concise and focused on specific topics, like scheduling a visit or following up after a game or tournament. Share only the necessary information they've asked for—no fluff or long introductions. Remember, college coaches may not have time for casual chats, so keep your messages relevant and to the point.

HIGHLIGHTS VIDEOS

A common mistake in recruiting is the length and style of highlight videos. College coaches receive a lot of video content, and they don't have time to watch multiple five-minute clips for every player. Videos don't need to look ultra-professional; fancy graphics, intro music, or elaborate edits aren't necessary. Coaches are primarily interested in seeing your skills in action, so aim to keep the video short—under a minute if possible—and focus on showcasing your strengths.

For hitters, show four to five swings in a training environment, followed by four to five solid game at-bats, and finish with some defensive highlights. If you're a pitcher, include four to five pitches in a game setting for each of your main pitches—fastballs, sliders, change-ups, etc. If you have good footage from training sessions, particularly with metrics like velocity and spin rate, include that as well.

METRICS REPORTS

Metrics reports are also increasingly valuable in recruitment, especially with the rise of training technology. These reports capture data on pitch or hit outcomes and can usually be exported as a PDF, making them easy to attach to an email. Many colleges now use these reports for player development and evaluation, so including them in your outreach can strengthen your profile.

Providing detailed metrics data to colleges is an excellent way to represent yourself in the recruiting process and helps distinguish you from other recruits who may not have access to similar technology. At KPI, we pride ourselves on supporting athletes throughout the recruiting journey. Our athletes not only benefit from exceptional training backed by advanced technology but also from the use of detailed technology reports, which significantly enhance their visibility in the recruiting process. This access to metrics is a key differentiator.

Metrics reports are often more valuable than high school stats. High school statistics can be misleading due to varying levels of competitiveness, which often don't match the intensity of college-level play. Success at the high school level doesn't always translate to success in college because the competition is far less rigorous. Colleges, however, understand and trust metrics data, which directly correlates to their level of play, making these reports a critical aspect of recruitment.

How to Create Effective Outreach for Colleges

- **Be concise and to the point.** Avoid unnecessary fluff; focus on essential details.
- **Provide everything they need upfront.** Ensure all relevant information is included in the first communication.
- **Include the following details:**
    - **Highlight video** (1 minute or less):
        - Include skill work, defensive plays, game clips, and training footage.
    - **Stats:**
        - High school and travel ball statistics.
    - **Contact information**:
        - High school coach, travel ball coach, and trainer details.
    - **Transcripts and test scores:**
        - Include SAT/ACT scores if available.
    - **Metrics:**
        - Key metrics like fastball velocity, exit velocity, and the 60-yard dash. Use videos or technology reports from reputable training facilities like KPI to validate the data.

CHOOSE A SIDE

UNDERSTANDING VISITS: UNOFFICIAL VS. OFFICIAL

As previously mentioned, the school does not cover unofficial visits financially. These visits are often for local athletes who can drive to the campus, and they don't require the school to process paperwork or cover travel costs. However, unofficial visits are still documented with the school's compliance office and the NCAA, signaling that they are indeed recruiting visits. These are typically one-day events where the athlete and their family meet with the coaching staff, tour the campus and facilities, and learn more about the program.

Official visits, in contrast, are much more structured. They require detailed reporting to the NCAA, including the athlete's NCAA ID number, and compliance offices must log and track the visit. The baseball program covers the costs of travel, meals, and any tickets for sporting events attended during the visit.

Observe the following factors when attending a college visit:

- **Dress appropriately.** While a suit isn't necessary, look professional and avoid sweats or hoodies.
- **Wear comfortable walking shoes.** Expect to tour the campus and facilities.
- **Prepare questions.** Have thoughtful questions about the program, campus, and academics ready to ask during the visit.
- **Demonstrate maturity.** Make eye contact, offer a firm handshake, and engage with confidence. Coaches will be evaluating your readiness to join their program.
- **Be the primary communicator.** Coaches want to interact with the player directly to assess their readiness and character. Don't allow anyone else to speak for you.

- **Speak professionally.** Avoid slang or informal terms like "bro" during the visit.

Official visits are often reserved for two scenarios. The first is during the recruiting process for athletes traveling to the school, particularly if they are from out of state. The second scenario, which is becoming more common, is when a school invites an entire class of verbally committed athletes to visit as a group in the fall. These weekend events are designed to build camaraderie and introduce the future class to the program before they sign financial aid agreements.

HOW TO TALK TO A COLLEGE COACH

The following are the strategies for effectively communicating with a college coach. First and foremost, treat them like normal people. College coaches are regular individuals, just like your high school and travel ball coaches. Talk to them in a casual, natural way, as you would to any adult in your life. They don't need overly formal speeches or rehearsed, ultra-structured conversations. What they're looking for is to connect with you on a personal level. They want to understand who you are as a real person, not the scripted version of yourself.

They don't want to talk to someone who has memorized lines or prepared answers in advance. They're trying to get to know you as a young man. It's essential to be yourself in these interactions. When speaking with college coaches—whether during calls or visits—the athlete should do the majority of the talking. This is a critical aspect of the recruiting process because it's an opportunity for the athlete to showcase who they are and make a positive impression.

Parents must resist the urge to dominate the conversation. This is one area where parental over-involvement can backfire. Parents often step in to ensure the "right" things are said, but this can hurt the athlete's chances. Colleges are primarily interested in the athlete, not the parents. They want to see the athlete take charge of the conversation, answer questions confidently, and look them in the eye.

When parents jump in too often during these conversations, it can leave a negative impression. Overzealous parental involvement can deter schools from pursuing an athlete further. There are numerous real-world examples of athletes whose parents tried to control the process too much, and it ended up costing the athlete their opportunity. In several cases, schools have communicated directly to us as advisors, saying they were no longer interested in recruiting an athlete because they didn't want to deal with overly involved parents.

Allowing athletes to handle these conversations on their own also prepares them for success at the college level. Guiding them through this process now ensures that they develop the communication and interpersonal skills they'll need when they reach college, where they'll have to navigate these situations independently. By coaching athletes to take the lead and speak for themselves, we help them build confidence and independence, skills that will serve them well throughout their college careers.

Here are some sample questions that can be included in a visit. The general strategy is to be as specific as you can be. You want to avoid vague, general answers:

- **Baseball-Related Questions**
    - What do you guys do in practice every day?
    - How do you develop your hitters/pitchers?
    - How do you use technology in the program?
    - What's the style of your coaching staff?
    - How much do you value the relationships with the players?
    - What is the background and involvement of the strength coach and athletic trainers?
- **Academic-Related Questions**
    - Do you have a mandatory study hall for the team?
    - What are the tutoring and academic resources for the players?
    - What happens to a player if they get a bad grade on their transcript?
    - Are there academic resources on the road while the team is traveling?
    - How does the coaching staff handle the situation of a mandatory class that interferes with practice?
- **Campus-Related Questions**
    - What are the food options on campus?
    - Do athletes get any special meals or fuel stations?
    - Where are the hangout areas on campus?
    - How many fans come to games?
    - How easy is it to get around campus?

HOW TO KNOW IF A SCHOOL ISN'T INTERESTED ANYMORE

Recognizing when a school has lost interest is another critical part of the process, and there are specific signs to look for to determine this.

Schools cast a pretty wide net early in the recruiting process, and then they get narrowed down as that process progresses further along. It's very common for a school to initially express interest in an athlete, only to move on for a variety of reasons. The following are strategies to recognize when a school is no longer interested.

No Offer: If a financial scholarship or roster spot offer doesn't come after weeks or months of communication, it's a strong sign the school is no longer pursuing you. Schools may say they want to "follow you in the future," which could indicate they want to monitor your progress. However, without an actual offer after a certain period, it's unlikely they are seriously considering you.

Less Follow-Up: If communication drops off—no texts, no personal emails, or no direct follow-ups—it's a red flag. When communication feels like you've been placed on a general email list, it's a sign the school has shifted focus away from you.

Vague Directives on Next Steps: Schools with genuine interest provide specific actions, such as "We'll offer you on this date" or "We need a response by this deadline." If communication becomes vague, it usually signals diminishing interest. A lack of clear direction on the next steps is a strong indicator that the school may no longer be seriously recruiting you.

We've seen examples where athletes ignored these signs due to their strong desire to attend a dream school. For instance, one athlete held out hope for a school that initially showed enthusiasm but eventually lost interest without making it clear. The athletes missed out on other opportunities because they failed to recognize these cues and move on, ultimately leaving them without the offers they could have secured elsewhere.

HOW TO KNOW IF A COLLEGE IS A GOOD FIT

Evaluating whether a college is the right fit involves several factors, all of which need to be considered carefully during the recruiting process. Each athlete and their family must weigh these elements to make an informed decision.

Athletics: Consider whether the school's baseball program aligns with your aspirations and whether you are good enough to compete at that level. Research the school's schedule to assess competitiveness, examine who they play, and evaluate their record. Look into how many players from the program advance to professional ranks, as well as the reputation of the coaching staff and their development approach. These factors can provide insight into whether the program meets your athletic goals.

Academics: Evaluate the school's academic standing to ensure it aligns with your priorities. Is it a state school, a University of California institution, or a private school? Does it offer the academic rigor and reputation you're looking for? If high academic standards are important to you, this may eliminate some schools from consideration.

Financials: Financial considerations are critical. While college baseball is gradually moving toward more full scholarship opportunities, it remains largely a partial scholarship sport. This means programs divide a set number of scholarships among their entire roster, leaving most players with partial coverage. Families should expect to cover part of the tuition and living expenses out of pocket.

Understanding the financial commitment is crucial to determining whether a school is a viable option.

The financial burden of attending college can vary significantly, ranging from several thousand dollars to tens of thousands of dollars annually, depending on the institution. Public universities tend to be less expensive, and the gap between a full scholarship and a partial scholarship may not be as significant. However, at private schools, this gap can be substantial, and families must consider whether the financial commitment is manageable. Questions like "Do we qualify for financial aid?" and "How much academic scholarship money can my son receive?" become critical in bridging that gap. Financial considerations are absolutely crucial to determining whether a school is a viable option.

Social Fit: The social environment is another key factor for athletes to evaluate. Social dynamics can vary greatly depending on the size and type of school. Larger schools often have robust athletic departments, complete with football games, basketball games, and a vibrant, highly social atmosphere surrounding athletics. Conversely, smaller schools—especially private institutions—may offer a quieter environment with less activity within the athletic department.

Athletes should also consider the broader social scene, including fraternities, sororities, and off-campus activities. Some campuses have a lively social scene with abundant extracurricular options, while others may be more subdued. Additionally, campus life itself can differ dramatically—some athletes may thrive in the bustling environment of a large public university, while others may prefer the intimate, quieter atmosphere of a smaller private college.

Location: Geographic location plays a major role in decision-making. The setting around the campus can significantly affect a student-athlete's experience. Is the school located in a bustling, urban inner-city environment with easy access to restaurants, bars, and entertainment? Or is it in a quieter, more rural area where outdoor activities and open spaces predominate?

Some schools offer a coastal, beach-town vibe that may appeal to certain athletes, while others are situated in tight-knit communities that lack the traditional "college town" feel. It's important to assess whether the campus's surrounding area aligns with the athlete's personal preferences and lifestyle.

Coaching Style: Finally, understanding the coaching staff's style and reputation is critical. Families should research whether the coaching staff is known for developing players at a high level. What is the track record of this program? What have they accomplished in the past, and how do they help players reach their potential? Evaluating the coaching staff's ability to develop talent and support athletes is an essential step in determining whether the program is a good fit.

What's their style? That can range from being very laid back and player-friendly to a little bit more hardcore, in-your-face style. How does the athlete respond to some of those different coaching styles? What is that coaching staff's reputation? Is that a match? These are important considerations to bear in mind.

Technology: Finally, the use of technology in college baseball programs is an important topic to consider. There is a common misconception that all colleges in the baseball world employ technology at a high level, but this is far from true. In fact, most colleges do not use technology extensively. If an athlete values the technological aspects of development and evaluation, they need to research different college baseball programs to determine whether a particular college incorporates technology in its approach.

At KPI, where technology plays a central role, we often need to advise athletes about this disparity. Growing up in our technology-driven environment can make it seem like the norm, so we make a point of letting them know that many college programs operate differently. We ask them to consider whether they'd be OK with a program that doesn't emphasize technology in the same way. This is particularly relevant for athletes in our program, as it can be a significant factor in their decision-making process.

In summary, recognizing when a school is no longer interested and evaluating whether a college is the right fit are essential parts of the recruiting process. These considerations help athletes and their families make sound, well-informed decisions that balance athletic, academic, and financial priorities.

To recap, here are the main factors that should be considered when evaluating the fit of a college for a young athlete:

- **Athletic:** Does this school fit what I am looking for athletically as a player?
- **Facilities:** Are the facilities what I am looking for?
- **Academics:** Do the academic standards meet my criteria?
- **Financial:** Does the financial offer fit what my family can afford?
- **Social:** Does the campus life and surrounding area fit what I want out of my college experience?
- **Developmental Tools:** Do they have the technology and approach to make me a better ballplayer and potentially get me to the professional level?

Taking all these factors into consideration will give you a good chance of ensuring that you identify a program that matches your needs and expectations to give you the best opportunity to maximize the benefits of your college experience. In the following chapter, we'll explore the ultimate goal of the recruiting process: making the final decision as to which college to attend.

CHAPTER 10

MAKING A DECISION

The choice of which college to attend is truly a life-shaping decision. It's usually the most intense decision a young ballplayer will make until they are well into adulthood. If a player has the opportunity to choose between colleges, they have successfully navigated the challenging recruiting process. Now comes the difficult task of making the final decision. This requires careful thought, a structured plan for evaluating all aspects of the process, and a clear focus on the priorities that each family deems most important.

High-level facilities like KPI and certain travel programs offer systematic processes to assist families with this decision. Like other parts of the developmental journey, this decision-making process should be guided by structure, clarity, and the expertise of those with substantial experience in the field.

STEP 1: SELF-ASSESSMENT

The first step in making a decision during the recruiting process is to perform an honest self-assessment. Take stock of where you are now and consider what level you could realistically reach. These may not be the same, so you will need to balance your current status with your potential as you move forward. Start by relying on data and metrics.

If you've done your homework and have access to advanced metrics, you should know where you stand, including your strengths, deficiencies, and how you compare to athletes at the college level. This data can help you evaluate whether there is a significant gap between your current abilities and the average player at your desired level. It also allows you to assess whether incremental improvements can bring you closer to meeting the expectations of a particular school. Metrics offer a clear and objective picture of where you stand now and where you might be in the future.

STEP 2: EVALUATE THE MARKET

It's also essential to consider the types of schools that have shown interest in you. If your dream schools—those large, prestigious programs—haven't recruited you or extended offers, it may be time to adjust your expectations. Align your focus with the schools that are actively recruiting you. This will help you develop a realistic understanding of your opportunities and refine your goals to match your current position in the process.

STEP 3: SEEK OUTSIDE PERSPECTIVE

Leverage your network for valuable insights. Your high school coach, travel ball coach, and trainer can provide different perspectives on your abilities and potential. These individuals may also have inside knowledge about the schools recruiting you, including their programs, coaching styles, and overall environments. Engaging in open conversations with your network can help you make a more informed decision.

STEP 4: BE REALISTIC

After analyzing your metrics and evaluating the schools that are showing interest, it's time to face the reality of your situation. If your dream schools aren't aligning with your current status, it makes sense to adjust your expectations. The good news is that those dream schools don't necessarily guarantee a great experience or a successful baseball career. In fact, such schools often have highly competitive and cutthroat environments, where many players end up leaving.

Focus on the opportunities that are in front of you. As the saying goes, "The grass is greener where you water it." Embrace the options you have, knowing that with effort and the right attitude, you can thrive. Remember, the transfer portal provides an opportunity to leave a program that ultimately doesn't feel like the right fit, so your first decision doesn't have to be final.

It's always crucial to gather as much information as possible from the people who know you best and get their perspectives while also understanding that the final decision will ultimately be yours. When talking to your network, ask if any of your coaches have direct connections to the colleges or college coaches recruiting you. Their insights can be invaluable. Ask them about their perceptions of the coaches as people and about their strengths and weaknesses.

This approach will give you access to insider information that you might not be able to uncover on your own. Your coaches may have valuable perspectives on these programs and their staff. Additionally, speak to both current and former players in the programs recruiting you. This step is essential during recruiting visits—try to have conversations with athletes currently in the program. These players are typically candid and honest about their experiences. If you can contact former players, their insights are equally important, as they no longer have any incentive to withhold or distort the truth. They'll likely give you an honest assessment of the program, the coaches, and whether it could be a good fit for you.

SPECIFIC QUESTIONS TO ASK:

Ask targeted questions about the coaching style and how development is approached for your position. For example:

- If you're a hitter, ask, "How do you develop hitters? What's your hitting philosophy?"
- If you're a pitcher, ask about their approach to pitching development.

If academics are important to you, inquire about the academic support the program provides. Ask questions like:

- "How do you manage study halls?"
- "What resources do you offer for students struggling academically?"
- "Do you provide tutoring?"

These specific questions will help you gain deeper insight into how the program aligns with your personal priorities.

PRIORITIZE AND RANK FACTORS:

At this stage, creating a comprehensive list of priorities and ranking them can help clarify your decision. Refer to the factors mentioned in Chapter 9—athletics, academics, financials, social life, location, coaching style, and technology. Write these down for each school you're considering, whether on paper or in a notes app, and rank them based on your individual and family priorities.

For some families, academics might outweigh athletics, making the academic reputation of the school a dominant factor. For others, athletics may take precedence, particularly if the player's primary goal is to pursue a professional career. This emphasis can significantly influence how the evaluation process unfolds. Every family will have its own unique context and values, so listing and ranking these factors is essential to ensuring that decisions are made in alignment with what truly matters to you.

BEWARE OF THE "PERFECT FIT" TRAP

One common pitfall is the belief that there's a perfect fit out there. It's important to remember that no option will be flawless. Every school, program, or situation will have its strengths and weaknesses.

This reality underscores the importance of evaluating your options objectively, ranking priorities, and making an informed decision based on the best fit for your specific goals and needs.

Sometimes, when you write stuff down on paper in this decision-making process, the athlete and the family want the choice to check every box. There will never be a situation where a school is a perfect fit, checking every single box. Instead, this evaluation process is more about assessing how many boxes a school checks and how well that aligns with the priorities you've set for the college experience you want. Remember, it's not about finding a flawless match but about identifying the school that best meets the majority of your needs and goals.

TAKE YOUR TIME AND DON'T RUSH

This is crucial: Don't commit right after a visit or a phone call. Recency bias can easily sway decisions. Often, athletes make multiple recruiting visits over several weeks or months. As they progress through these visits, they might start to favor the most recent one, remembering only the highlights and forgetting the positive aspects of earlier visits.

To counter this, document your priorities, pros, and cons after each visit. Capture your feelings about each school immediately so that when the time comes to make a decision, you have an objective record of your initial impressions. After the final visit, give yourself two to four weeks to let the shine of that last visit fade. This approach enables a more balanced and objective decision based on your documented priorities rather than on the excitement of a recent visit.

ENSURE IT'S THE BEST FIT, NOT JUST THE HIGHEST-RANKED SCHOOL

Many athletes and their families aim for the biggest, most prestigious school, assuming it will offer the best experience. However, larger schools often bring a more competitive, high-stakes environment that may prioritize winning over individual development. These larger programs tend to over-recruit and cut down later, and they are more likely to invest heavily in transfers through the transfer portal. This creates a highly competitive and cutthroat atmosphere, which can sometimes prioritize results over the growth and well-being of the individual athlete.

While these schools have strong brand recognition, they may not always be the best fit. There are numerous examples, including personal cases we've observed, where athletes chose a high-profile school based solely on its name. Once they arrived, they found themselves feeling like a small fish in a big pond, struggling to stand out. This experience often leads to transferring, being cut, or simply starting over at a smaller school. In the current context—specifically, considering the role of the transfer portal—athletes might benefit more from starting at a smaller school where they can have early on-field success, receive more development opportunities, and potentially play a significant role from the start. If they rise to the level of a bigger school later in their college career, they can take advantage of the transfer portal and the increased flexibility that exists today to make that move when the timing is right.

ORGANIZING THOUGHTS TO MAKE THE FINAL DECISION

At the very end of the recruiting process, one of the most effective ways to organize your thoughts and make a decision is by using a simple pros and cons T-chart. Start by listing out your top priorities. Then, for each school you're considering, populate the chart with how well it meets each priority. This visual comparison can facilitate a structured family discussion, bringing everyone closer to a consensus and helping to achieve peace of mind about the decision.

HOW TO COMMIT

Here are the steps to take when committing to a school to ensure you do so properly. Many athletes and their families overlook important parts of this process, which can lead to hard feelings among the colleges they decline and may even affect the athlete's broader recruiting network.

1. **Inform the School You're Committing To.** The first and most essential step is to call the school you've chosen. It doesn't necessarily have to be the head coach; reach out to the coach you've had the most interaction with or developed the strongest relationship with during the recruiting process. Let them know that you are committing to their program. Keep the conversation clear, positive, and straightforward.
2. **Notify Other Schools.** The next step, though uncomfortable, is to contact the other schools that invested time in recruiting you. Let them know you will not be attending their program. This step is often skipped

because it's hard for a high school athlete to call a college coach and deliver this news. However, it's a necessary part of doing things the right way. It reflects maturity and respect for the time and effort those coaches spent on you. When making these calls, keep the conversation professional and brief. You can say something like, *"I appreciate the time and effort you've put into recruiting me. After careful consideration, I've decided to attend [School Name]."* If the coach asks for further explanation, you can share as much as you feel comfortable with, but your primary obligation is to deliver the decision clearly and respectfully. If the coach does not answer, leave a polite voicemail with a similar message. Once you've made this communication, you are not obligated to answer follow-up calls from that school.

3. **Avoid Texting or Emailing for Declining Offers.** Do not communicate this decision via text or email. Taking the time to make a phone call shows maturity and acknowledges the effort the coach put into recruiting you. It's a small but significant gesture of respect and professionalism.

HOW TO ANNOUNCE YOUR COMMITMENT ON SOCIAL MEDIA

A social media post announcing your commitment is a great way to share the news with your community and peers. To make it stand out, consider creating a professional-looking graphic. You can find graphic design services on platforms like Instagram or Twitter, where there are accounts that specialize in creating commitment graphics for a small fee. This can elevate the announcement and give it a polished, celebratory look.

In your caption, you want to express your excitement—and if you're religious, even your sense of being blessed—to be committing to that school. Start with a general thank-you to everyone who has supported you, such as friends, family, former coaches, and others along those lines. Then, give a special thanks to those who have been more intimately involved in your journey. If a specific coach has greatly influenced you or helped you through the process, name them. If you have an advisor who has been particularly supportive or a trainer with whom you share a deep connection, give them a special mention, along with your parents at this point in time.

End with an action statement about helping the school achieve its mission. For example, if you picked up on a particular goal the school has during the recruiting process, such as winning a national championship or securing their conference, reference that at the end of your post. Be sure to include hashtags for the college, the team, and the athletic department to attract followers.

These colleges often have strong social media followings, and people who support the school will likely start following you. Building a large following now could potentially bring financial benefits down the road. Using the school's hashtag is crucial, as it allows followers of their account to discover you as a future student-athlete. Additionally, tag your high school team, your travel team, and your college team. If you train at a specific facility, tag that as well. This boosts your post in the algorithm, providing those entities the chance to repost your content, as everyone will take pride in your commitment.

CHAPTER 11

PHYSICAL DEVELOPMENT, BALANCE, AND TRAINING

The journey of getting to and performing at the collegiate level does not end at the verbal commitment or signing. Rather, the difficult part of this journey has just begun. It takes an incredible amount of effort to step onto a college campus on the first day of fall, fully prepared to compete at the collegiate level. In today's world of "drops" and de-commitments, colleges now expect athletes to show both physical and mental growth. Physical development should be the top priority, and athletes should also begin preparing for independent living. Learning practical skills like doing laundry, cooking, and cleaning can be extremely valuable during this phase, even though they are often overlooked. The less adjustment to independent life the athlete needs, the better for their performance.

At KPI, we use this phase to get highly specific with training. With the college commitment already secured, we leverage our technology and staff to pinpoint precise areas where the athlete needs improvement. We then combine this with feedback from the college's coaching staff on their expectations to create a highly targeted, detailed program. Our approach prioritizes health, as a serious injury can be a key reason why a player's college commitment might be jeopardized.

Balancing training and playing is essential after the commitment. Once committed to a college, it's easy to focus on seeking more exposure and evaluation, letting training take a back seat. Athletes often get comfortable in their new status as a recent college commit, coasting by and opting for what feels easy.

Some pitfalls at this stage include attending too many tournaments in pursuit of exposure. This can strain them physically, as they reduce their training time and put physical development on hold simply because playing feels more enjoyable. Overloading on games can, however, jeopardize their commitment by undermining the physical progression colleges expect to see at this stage. Colleges want athletes to balance training and playing. They discourage playing 100 games a year without training, as they know this won't bridge the gap between the athlete's current physical state and the level needed to compete in college. Playing too much and reaching a state of fatigue often leads to an increased risk of injury or a notable drop in performance. Maintaining a balance is critical at this point.

This balance remains crucial for success at the next level. Physical training is a major part of being a college athlete, and there are times throughout the college athletic calendar when training will take priority over skill development. Colleges want athletes to start displaying this balance at the high school level as they transition from a college commitment to becoming a college athlete. Injuries during the recruiting process can significantly complicate matters.

This is another important reason not to deprioritize training:

Training helps keep you healthy. If you're committed to a college and suffer a serious injury, that college then faces a tough decision —whether they believe you'll be fully healthy by the time you arrive. An injury could complicate or even jeopardize your commitment status with them. College coaches are essentially paid to win games, so if they doubt your ability to help them achieve that due to potential injuries or setbacks, they might reconsider honoring their commitment to you because of concerns about your health. Additionally, it becomes challenging for colleges to evaluate where you stand in the recruiting process, especially as you near attendance. If you're injured, they can't be certain of your status.

Colleges may hesitate to follow through on a commitment if they have to guess whether you'll be healthy and ready for their level. You need to consistently progress physically to be prepared for both college and professional competition. The focus should always be on physical readiness for the next level. Skill work has its place, but physicality is paramount. The longer the physical gap remains, the less time the college has to determine if you can compete at their level. They are constantly evaluating you in comparison with other recruits. They're going to be asking themselves, "Does this committed player measure up to the other high school players we're considering?"

Training also builds the physical resilience necessary to stay healthy throughout a baseball career. The college schedule is demanding, so developing physical capacity and preparing the body for this rigor early can be extremely valuable. A player's body and mind will be tested in unique ways as soon as they set foot on campus, so preparation should start well in advance of their arrival.

A key to staying motivated and engaged during this phase is setting a series of goals. There should be training goals, performance goals, and personal goals aimed at making you better prepared to compete when you arrive at college in the fall. Athletes should work with their coaches, trainers, committed college, and family to establish goals across all these areas. The following are some examples of some good goals to set to better prepare to show up to college:

- **Training:** Set a velocity goal for pitching, a body weight goal, a movement goal for an off-speed pitch, an exit velocity or bat speed goal for a hitter, and some strength/force goals in some specific lifts.
- **Performance:** Set some goals for playing with travel teams, some objective statistic goals for both travel and high school teams, and some end-of-season reward goals for high school (MVP, All-League, etc.).
- **Personal:** Learn how to do laundry, learn how to cook, learn how to vacuum, etc.

If there's a large physical gap between where you are and where they want you to be, then eventually, the college you're committed to might shift their attention towards that other athlete that doesn't have that large of a physical gap. There are some well-known case studies and examples of this. A recent example involves a young man who, in the early stages of high school, was highly sought after by many top schools. He was tall and slender, had a good arm, and was seen as a promising long-term athlete. Many colleges offered him spots, and he committed to a prestigious school. However, by the fall of his senior year, his physical condition was largely the same as before: He was still a decent high school pitcher, but he hadn't developed physically since his sophomore year. As a result, the college he'd been committed to for over a year decided to drop him due to his lack of physical progress. He then had to scramble to find a new school, ultimately ending up at a much smaller, less accomplished program than his initial commitment.

At this stage, another useful strategy is to align with the college recruitment calendar to help set your playing schedule. Colleges have certain periods in the year for recruiting, which include contact phases when they can scout and dead phases when they can't (this is discussed earlier in the book, in Chapter 8). I strongly recommend aligning your playing calendar with these phases, as it mirrors the annual cadence colleges use with their own teams. This structure can guide when an athlete should focus on competition and when to prioritize physical training.

PART FOUR

POST-COMMITMENT PHASE

CHAPTER 12

THE TIME BETWEEN THE COMMITMENT AND GETTING TO CAMPUS

The period of time between the college commitment and getting to campus (or professional baseball) can often be the most consequential stretch in a young ballplayer's career and progression to the highest levels of the game. There must be a fierce focus and unwavering dedication to development, with an obsession for being fully prepared on day one of attending fall classes. As the transition from high school to college player unfolds, a great deal of nuance is required in training and preparation.

At KPI, having trained and guided numerous athletes to collegiate and professional levels, we know how to prepare them physically and mentally for this critical stage.

A typical timeline begins once an athlete commits, which can happen as early as the beginning of their junior year or, more commonly, during their senior year in the fall. There are several key milestones in this process that should be highlighted. One such milestone is the official visit. At larger colleges, especially those with football programs, these visits often involve bringing in the entire recruiting class for the following year. Typically held in the fall, this weekend event serves to initiate bonding among the recruits and acclimate them to the school environment. Activities often include staying in a hotel, having team meals or meals with the recruiting class, socializing with the current team, and attending a football game. This bonding experience is a highlight for many athletes and plays a significant role in transitioning to college life.

Another common milestone in the past was the signing day, traditionally held in the second week of November under the previous National Letter of Intent (NLI) system. On this day, athletes would often hold a ceremony at their high school to sign their scholarship and NLI, officially committing to their college.

However, in October 2024, the NCAA abolished the NLI, replacing it with an institution-based system. Colleges now issue financial aid agreements to their commitments at any point during the athlete's senior year. This change has shifted responsibility to the institutions, allowing them to decide when and how to issue agreements and make them binding. While this process is less formal than the old signing day, the financial aid agreement now serves as the official commitment document, though it may not be legally binding until the athlete attends classes. This shift makes it even more critical for athletes to continue physical development, as colleges now have greater flexibility to evaluate and adjust their incoming roster up until the new class arrives in the fall.

After completing their senior year, many colleges prefer their incoming freshmen to play summer ball or arrive early on campus for summer school classes and training. This approach offers numerous benefits. It allows incoming freshmen to begin their transition to independence with a "soft opening." During the summer, campuses are typically quieter, providing recruits with a chance to adjust to campus life, establish routines, and acclimate to the structure of college without the distractions of a fully populated campus. This low-pressure environment is ideal for building confidence and preparing for the challenges of college life.

The same concept applies to why colleges encourage many incoming players to participate in summer ball. This allows them to leave home, begin experiencing independence, and adjust to that side of their life, which is a dramatic transition. Additionally, it provides a more challenging level of competition in collegiate summer leagues compared to staying local. Often, some future teammates play on the same summer team, which helps accelerate the acclimation and bonding process necessary for success at the collegiate level.

Colleges also need to continue evaluating players during this final year of the process. They want assurance that the athlete will develop and contribute once on campus. This means they need to see physical progression and improvements in metrics, confirming that the athlete is consistently getting better. Without a binding document tying the college to the athlete, colleges retain flexibility for much longer now. If they find another available athlete who is better, they might choose to de-commit from their original recruit. This dynamic places considerable pressure on athletes to continue improving, ensuring the college feels confident about the verbal and financial commitment made between the two parties. As such, athletes must stay focused on their physical development and consistently demonstrate progress.

At this stage, it is crucial for athletes to train with reputable professionals rather than relying on random or low-level training programs. Once on campus, they will be immersed in a rigorous and professional environment, so their training during this final phase should reflect the standards and demands they will encounter.

For a select group of players, often during the fall of their senior year or even earlier, the process might include engagement with professional sports agents or advisors. If a player is talented enough to potentially be drafted by a Major League Baseball (MLB) team directly out of high school, it becomes necessary to employ an advisor to navigate this complex process. This advisor process can resemble the college recruiting process, with various professional agencies reaching out to schedule what are essentially sales meetings.

Typically, the athlete and their family will host home visits with different agencies, during which the agencies present their pitch on why they are the best choice for the athlete. After conducting a series of these meetings, the athlete will ultimately decide who they want as their advisor. For players at this level, the next step involves scout meetings during the winter and early spring. Local area scouts from MLB organizations visit the athlete's home to ask general questions about their personal life, training regimen, family background, and other relevant topics.

Choosing an advisor can be a daunting task for a family, as navigating through the professional baseball world is very intimidating. Families should definitely be guided by a trusted coach during this phase, as they will need someone in their corner who has the requisite experience and knowledge of this phase of the process. Advisors and agencies are professionals, and the industry is unregulated, so it is very easy to get confused and not know what to do.

The following are indications that you should get an advisor:

- You have been selected for ultra-elite individual events like Area Codes, Perfect Game All-American Games, or the USA Baseball Trials or Development Programs.
- Professional scouts of MLB organizations have started to reach out about opportunities and to build relationships.
- You are committed to or are being courted by major Top 25 universities and baseball programs.
- Reputable agencies have started to reach out to your "team" of coaches.
    - Small-time agencies that send cold DMs or wait for players after events without invitations should not be considered.

Here's what to look for in a potential advisor/agency:

- **MLB clients:** They have a large roster of clients in the major leagues. This signals that they have a real ability to guide you through the process properly.
- **Ability to help with NIL deals:** The advisor can now be a large part of the college commitment and NIL process. There should be a structured and established plan for securing the player NIL deals.
- **Clear philosophy on college vs. professional baseball:** Reputable agencies will almost always steer a player to go to college unless there is a consequential financial sum available in the draft out of high school. Smaller agencies are just trying to profit from a signing bonus, which means they will encourage players to sign for smaller amounts out of high school. This can often be

detrimental to their careers because it lowers their chances of making it to MLB.
- **Personality fit:** Different agencies have different philosophies, and the personalities of those involved will be distinctive. Families should get a feel for this in the meetings that take place and consider it in their decision-making.
- **Structure and size of the agency:** Reputable agencies range in size and structure. With smaller outfits, there will be a relationship and connection with the principals of the agency. Large agencies have employees assigned to the younger athletes, and those athletes will have very little to no connection to the actual agents in the agency.

If things become serious after the spring high school season of the senior year, Major League Baseball (MLB) teams may invite the athlete to a pre-draft workout. These are usually small or individual workouts held at the team's training complex or stadium, where the athlete undergoes a private evaluation.

After these pre-draft workouts, there is typically a quiet period during which agents discuss the athlete's potential signability with MLB organizations. These conversations center on whether there's alignment between the athlete's financial expectations and the projections MLB teams have for their value. By this stage, there's often a mutual understanding about whether the athlete will likely be selected in the draft. It's relatively uncommon for MLB teams to draft a player without confidence that the player is willing to sign, as they don't want to waste a draft pick.

Usually, these deals are more or less agreed upon before the draft takes place. In many cases, athletes are talented enough to be drafted, but the financial gap between what they expect to sign for and the amount MLB teams are prepared to offer is too wide. If an agreement isn't likely, MLB organizations typically won't draft the player, as failing to secure a signed commitment wastes their draft resources. This underscores how critical pre-draft negotiations are to the process.

At this stage, there are significant differences that athletes must consider, especially if they're talented enough to be drafted. The experiences of a college freshman on campus differ drastically from those of a professional player in the minor leagues.

College life, particularly at larger universities, is highly team-oriented. It's marked by vibrant campus activities, communal support, and a sense of shared purpose. Everyone, from teammates to coaches, is working toward a common goal. Relationships are central to the experience, and coaches are heavily invested in their players' success because winning games contributes to the overall vibrancy and prestige of the college community.

In contrast, the professional level operates very differently. While players are technically part of a team, the environment is highly individualistic. Everyone is focused on advancing to the major leagues, so players are primarily looking out for their own interests. The atmosphere is often isolating, with frequent travel and little emphasis on team bonding or communal activities. Success is largely self-driven, and the professional level can feel transactional, with relationships and support networks taking a backseat to individual performance and advancement.

It's not set up to ensure your success. For example, if you demonstrate that you're not good enough, you get injured a lot, or you're not living up to expectations, there won't be much support for you. The professional organization will consider you a business asset, and they can easily dispose of you if they feel that you're not a worthwhile asset to be holding.

CHAPTER 13

HOW TO KEEP YOUR COMMITMENT

Your commitment to a college is only the beginning of this process. Sustained development and achievement are what will prepare you to excel at the next levels of the game.

These are the strategies that need to be employed to ensure the athlete completes their senior year strong and arrives on campus ready to compete at the highest level, honoring their commitment. The goal is to close the physical gap. As explained earlier, colleges expect to see consistent physical progression and need to feel confident the athlete can make a positive impact on their program from day one. Athletes must identify the areas they need to address physically and ensure they are preparing themselves adequately to meet those demands.

A great strategy is to communicate directly with the college coaches about their expectations. Reach out to them and ask, "What do you want to see me improve on between now and when I arrive on campus?" Once you have their feedback, go all in on addressing those areas. For example, if they want you to run faster, improve arm strength, or throw harder, take that input seriously and focus on making those improvements.

By following through and making tangible progress, you'll show the coaches during evaluations—whether late in your senior year or upon arrival—that you've worked hard to meet their expectations. This can solidify your standing with the program. Another useful step is to analyze the team roster. Look at the physical attributes of current players—height, weight, and key metrics—and compare yourself to those benchmarks. For pitchers, check the velocity of the players in their program. If there's a noticeable gap between your stats and theirs, focus on closing that gap.

Using metrics and other evaluative tools to understand the program's standards can provide valuable insights. Aligning your development with these expectations will help ensure you're ready to compete on day one.

One of our long-time, ultra-high-level athletes provides a good example of this approach. This young man was a highly talented high school player who committed early to a major national powerhouse—a program recognized as one of the best in the country. During his senior year, we evaluated what he needed to improve on to compete physically from the moment he stepped on campus. We worked with the college he was committed to and his professional advisors to develop a developmental plan to maximize his draft value and be the most prepared if he did end up going to college. We determined that diversifying his pitch arsenal by adding a slider would be key. He worked diligently on developing the slider throughout his senior year. When he arrived on campus, the slider became his primary pitch, enabling him to make an immediate impact as a freshman. He earned first-team Freshman All-American honors, largely due to the advanced pitch arsenal he had developed during his senior year.

In addition to focusing on physical preparation, you should also continue playing at a high level. Demonstrate skill progression and perform consistently against top competition to show that you are improving and ready to take on collegiate challenges.

If your high school program is not at a high competitive level, you should seek higher-level play during the fall and in summer ball after your senior year to sharpen your skills and prepare for the elevated competition you'll face in college. This will help ensure you aren't caught off guard or overwhelmed by the level of play during your freshman fall season. Additionally, you'll want to mimic the college playing schedule to adapt to their annual cadence.

Colleges don't typically play 30–40 games in the fall. Instead, they focus on inter-squad games and may play against another team once or twice. Your schedule should reflect this by limiting your games to 10–15 in the fall, just as colleges do. Similarly, take the winter off from competition to prioritize training, which aligns with the collegiate offseason.

During your senior year, play the most games in the spring. In the summer, find a balance between playing and training. For pitchers who threw a lot of innings in the spring, it may be wiser to rest and train during the summer to ensure you're physically ready for fall. Position players who need more at-bats to prepare for higher-level competition should work with their college coaches to determine the right balance of summer games and training to maximize physical readiness.

Academics remain critically important even after a commitment has been made and a financial aid agreement signed. After graduating high school, you'll need to send your final transcripts to the college you're committed to. If your transcripts don't meet the admissions requirements, you could face significant problems and may not be admitted to the school.

To avoid this, have early conversations during your senior year about the academic standards your college expects. Determine the GPA, test scores, and class schedule necessary for admission. If you're falling short, consider hiring tutors to help you meet these standards. Taking these steps ensures you align academically with what the college requires and secures your place in the program.

Very often, academics are overlooked after a commitment or financial aid agreement is signed. However, one of the final steps in the process is for the school to admit you based on your senior year academic performance. It's not uncommon for players to fall short of the school's requirements, leaving them scrambling at the last minute. To avoid this, it is essential to maintain focus on academics throughout your senior year.

Another critical aspect of honoring your commitment and following through in your senior year is training. Use technology to identify weaknesses and address them objectively. Research the average metrics of college players at the level you're entering. For example, if you're heading to a top 25 Division I program, find out the metrics of those players and use your senior year to develop yourself to align with those standards. If your commitment is to a program at a slightly lower level, the same concept applies—study what players at that level are achieving and focus on closing any physical gaps.

Make it a priority to get as strong and prepared as possible for college competition. This also shows your commitment to the school, demonstrating visible progress and proving that you're willing to work hard to meet their expectations.

Athletes should establish weekly and monthly goals and create a checklist to track their progress. This system can begin as soon as the commitment is made and continue until the athlete arrives on campus. Setting regular, achievable milestones ensures that every area of need is addressed, with the ultimate goal of being fully prepared for the collegiate level by fall. This approach not only boosts motivation but also ensures a thorough and methodical preparation process.

At KPI, we excel during this stage of development because we've successfully sent many athletes to the college level. We have extensive data on what players need to do to be ready, and we tailor individualized programs for each athlete. This allows them to target their weaknesses effectively and ensure they are fully prepared to compete at the collegiate level.

CHAPTER 14

WHAT TO EXPECT AT THE COLLEGE LEVEL

The transition from high school to college athletics is typically a dramatic change and introduces a vastly different environment for the athlete. It's essential for athletes to understand what to expect at this level, as the experience can often be overwhelming during the fall of their freshman year. This period is commonly a time when athletes get off track if they're not prepared, so understanding what to expect can help prevent this.

One of the first factors to anticipate at the college level is the intensity of the competition. The initial adjustment for a player involves understanding that the expectations for their habits and performance are much higher than in high school. Every aspect of their life—practicing, performing, training, academics, and even social interactions—is more demanding. Additionally, a highly paid coaching staff is invested in winning, creating an environment with increased expectations and little tolerance for underperformance. Many athletes struggle to adapt to this, which is why practicing independence before leaving for college is crucial. Athletes who are overly dependent upon arrival often face setbacks, which can slow their progression.

In high school, many players excelled with little internal competition on their team. At the college level, they will encounter fierce competition, not just against other teams but also within their own team. They must quickly adjust to the reality of battling for every opportunity. Every repetition in practice is evaluated, and athletes are either winning or losing that rep against their teammates. At the college level, everyone is talented, and the battle for playing time is intense. This adjustment involves competing for playing time during practice, not just games, and it is significant for young athletes.

The daily routine of a college athlete is highly demanding and structured, resembling a full-time job and often exceeding the hours of a typical full-time position. For example, the day might start at 5 a.m., with weightlifting or conditioning sessions beginning around 5:30 or 6 a.m. Afterward, athletes shower, grab a quick breakfast, and head to classes, followed by a four-hour practice session. Following practice, there may be study hall, dinner, and homework to complete before the day ends. Days are long and packed and leave little room for other activities, which can be stressful and overwhelming for those unaccustomed to such a schedule. Setting the expectation that college athletics will be long and challenging is vital.

Physical training is another significant adjustment. Most colleges employ full-time strength coaches whose sole focus is the athletes' physical development. For many young athletes, this is an entirely new experience. They are often used to training independently or with minimal guidance. College strength coaches are highly focused and expect substantial progress in physical strength and conditioning. These training sessions often occur early in the morning, which may be unfamiliar to young athletes.

Adapting to early morning sessions requires athletes to develop new habits, such as waking up earlier, eating breakfast early, and preparing for class after an intense workout. Learning to manage sleep, nutrition, and the demands of rigorous physical training is critical to thriving in this new environment.

There is also a high expectation for performance. Athletes are required to perform not only in games but also in practice environments. Coaches are often evaluated based on their win-loss record, which creates a constant atmosphere of pressure for which young athletes must be prepared. They cannot afford to coast during practice; their performance is scrutinized in every aspect of their participation. This performance pressure can lead to significant social and psychological adjustments for athletes, and many struggle to cope with it. For this reason, athletes should not be coddled or shielded from stress and pressure during high school, as exposure to these challenges helps them embrace and navigate the demands they will face at the college level.

Another adjustment involves the coach-player relationship, which can be vastly different from what athletes experience in high school or travel ball. This dynamic often depends on the personalities of the coaching staff, but it is generally more businesslike and less personal. At the high school and travel ball levels, the stakes are usually lower, and the atmosphere more casual, fostering more organic and nurturing relationships. At the collegiate level, however, the intense pressure to perform is ever-present, and most coaching staffs adopt a results-driven approach, often at the expense of emotional support. This lack of empathy can create a disconnect between players and coaches. Athletes should seek out coaches on staff who have a softer or more relatable approach to establish a supportive and constructive relationship. These will often be the younger coaches, but not necessarily. There is often the opportunity to connect with members of campus outside of the team, like tutors, trainers, clubs, etc. These relationships outside of the team environment can be crucial to providing the necessary balance and support for the player.

Freshmen entering college also face a stark shift in their living situation. They move from the comfort and oversight of home, where parents typically handle many responsibilities and provide constant guidance, to an environment where they are entirely on their own. Suddenly, these young athletes have complete freedom to make decisions without parental oversight, which makes their ability to make sound choices and exercise maturity immensely important. This newfound independence requires them to navigate various situations responsibly, as they now have full control over their actions and decisions.

Balancing a social life with the rigorous schedule of a college athlete is another key challenge. Many freshmen struggle with this balance when given newfound freedom, sometimes prioritizing their social life over their athletic and academic commitments. This imbalance can lead to significant trouble, as poor decision-making often has serious consequences. These consequences may include disciplinary action from the coaching staff, suspension by the athletic department or school, or even being cut from the team. Such outcomes are not uncommon for young athletes who fail to maintain the necessary focus and structure in their schedules.

Creating a block schedule where athletes plan out what they will do and when across their various responsibilities is a great strategy for managing the dynamics of their new lives. The following is an example of a block schedule for a college baseball player:

- 5:00–6:00 a.m.: Strength Session Preparation
  - Wake up, have breakfast, and leave enough time to ensure arrival prior to start time for strength training
- 6:00–7:00 a.m.: Strength Training
- 7:00–8:00 a.m.: Shower, get ready for classes, eat, arrive to class early
- 8:00–12:00 p.m.: Classes and Academic Time
  - Attend all classes, use any free time for studying or academic preparation
- 12:00–2:00 p.m.: Practice Preparation
  - Early hitting/defense/arm care work, athletic training time, field prep
- 2:00–5:00 p.m.: Baseball Practice
- 5:00–6:30 p.m.: Relaxation and Dinner
- 6:30–8:00 p.m.: Academic Time
  - Any homework, papers that need to be written, online class assignments, or getting ahead on future assignments
- 8:00–9:30 p.m.: Social/Family Time
  - Call home, hangout with friends

There are very serious consequences at this stage if an athlete doesn't know how to handle themselves properly. As noted previously, the overarching theme to understand in this context is that college coaches are paid to win games. Their primary job is to develop their team and achieve victories. If an athlete struggles significantly with the transition to college life and doesn't appear to offer the coach a real opportunity to help the team win games, it can jeopardize the coach's career. Ultimately, their livelihood depends on their ability to succeed, and losing too many games could cost them their job.

This is why coaches can be extremely tough on athletes. For them, it's not just about mentoring players—it's about maintaining their job security. If an athlete is slacking off, partying excessively, or neglecting their academics to the point that it impacts their on-field performance, the coach's ability to achieve victories is directly affected. Coaches do not take such infractions lightly and often deal with these issues in a cutthroat manner. They are under constant pressure to protect their positions, and they expect their athletes to demonstrate the same level of commitment.

CHAPTER 15

WHAT TO EXPECT AT THE PROFESSIONAL LEVEL

The jump to the professional level is daunting for any player, but especially those coming directly out of high school. Being on their own, enduring long days, lacking social time, and often facing substandard living conditions can wreak havoc on a freshly graduated 18-year-old, both physically and mentally. Everything is self-directed, and nothing is done for them. They are thrown into an ultra-competitive, real-world environment at a very young age.

At KPI, we implement some specialized programs to help athletes transition to pro ball. On top of their normal physical training, we try to educate them on proper sleep and nutrition programs. Part of our normal training with high-level athletes is to teach them proper self-care, soft tissue strategies, and arm care. These are valuable skills they are able to implement on their own in the professional environment.

For those who are fortunate enough to move on to the professional level, whether it's out of high school or out of college, there is a lifestyle adjustment. There's going to be a very different setup for a professional athlete compared to a college or high school athlete because you remove academics from the calendar, which is obviously a big part of any high school or college environment. Now the player moves out of what would be a rookie ball or short-season ball, which is usually based at the team's complex.

Once they get into the actual progression of the minor leagues, there are usually long bus rides. Because the budgets are very low, teams mostly can't afford to fly to many of the games, so lengthy bus rides are the norm. Very often, a team can play at six or seven o'clock at night and then take an all-night bus ride somewhere else. The player is expected to sleep on the bus and eat a quick meal; it's really a tough environment to develop physically. It's mentally challenging, and poor nutrition, late nights, and lack of sleep are common. These factors can combine to make it a real shock to the system, but it is fairly normal at the professional level.

There are also usually much lower living standards than what the player had at the college level. Especially for players who go to a major Division I college, the facility standards, the school-provided meals, and all the amenities that big schools offer aren't always there at the professional level. There aren't nice facilities, especially because they're on the road so much. For example, they will not have access to technology or upscale weight rooms that a facility like KPI or a good college would have. They're often just piecing their physical development together. They have to stay in cheap hotels, not usually in their own beds; it's not a very glamorous or high-end lifestyle, and it's really hard to perform and stay healthy.

There is also intense competition among individuals on the team. While the college environment is still very team-oriented—

even though the competition for playing time is fierce—the professional level is a very individual environment. Each player is trying to move their way up the minor league system and get to the major leagues, and that usually is not determined at all by the team's success. This makes it a very individualistic environment. Each player is primarily focused on their own progression and advancements. This "me first" mindset, centered on individual goals rather than a team-first approach, can be a dramatic change for many athletes.

Additionally, the mental grind of professional baseball represents a stark difference from earlier levels and can present significant challenges. The long schedule, which is vastly different from what most athletes are accustomed to, can be extremely demanding. Minor league players regularly play over 140 games a year, far more than they likely experienced before. Players dream of advancing to the professional level, and once they get there, they learn the mental and emotional toll it takes on them. It is essential that athletes navigating professional baseball develop and lean on their support system to help them through their career progression. It is also valuable to compile a collection of resources to help with their mental health or even hire a mental skills specialist. For the players that have agents, it is commonplace for professional agents to assist with these things.

There is very little wholesome social interaction with family and friends. Athletes spend most of their professional season on the road, depriving them of nurturing, positive social interactions with loved ones. This absence of close connections can be tough for young athletes. Moreover, unlike the highly structured and consistent college environment, the professional setting is marked by irregularity. Athletes are constantly traveling—moving from city to city, facility to facility, park to park, and hotel to hotel. This lack of consistency can be a major shock to their system, as it affects their routine and can seriously impact their development and performance.

The best players at the minor league and professional levels are those who are highly adaptable. They understand the varying demands of different environments and adopt a "chameleon" mindset, adjusting efficiently to changes. Athletes who are overly rigid and heavily dependent on their own routines often struggle in this setting. Their inability to adapt prevents them from maintaining the consistency needed for success, making it difficult to thrive in a constantly changing and unpredictable environment.

The following tips and techniques will help you adapt to this disruptive and potentially disorienting environment.

The Minor League Baseball Survival Guide

1. Recovery and Physical Maintenance

- **Foam Roller & Mini Massage Gun:** Essential for working out muscle stiffness after long bus rides and strenuous games.
- **Resistance Bands:** Lightweight and perfect for mobility work, stretching, and maintaining strength on the road.
- **Theracane or Massage Stick:** Handy for self-massage, particularly for reaching shoulder, back, and neck areas.
- **Compression Socks:** Helps reduce swelling and improve circulation during long bus rides.

- **Stretching Strap:** Compact and great for deeper stretches before or after games.
- **Lacrosse Ball or Tennis Ball:** Excellent for myofascial release, allowing you to work out knots and trigger points in smaller muscle areas.

2. Nutrition and Hydration

- **High-Protein Snacks:** Include protein bars, beef jerky, or single-serving packs of nuts to maintain energy and support muscle recovery.
- **Electrolyte Powder or Tablets:** Staying hydrated is crucial, especially after a day in the sun or traveling. Electrolyte supplements help replenish salts lost through sweat.
- **Meal Prep Containers & Cutlery:** If you have access to a fridge or want to pack meals, having containers on hand can save money and keep you on track nutritionally.
- **Portable Blender or Shaker Bottle:** For quick smoothies or protein shakes on the go.
- **Multivitamins or Nutrition Powders:** It's tough to get fresh food on the road, so it's crucial to ensure you take in essential vitamins and nutrients.
- **Nut Butter Packets:** Compact and nutrient-dense, these are great for quick, healthy calories.
- **Instant Oatmeal Packets:** Easy to prepare anywhere with hot water and can be customized with nuts, fruit, or protein powder for a balanced meal.

3. Sleep Aids and Comfort

- **Neck Pillow, Eye Mask, and Earplugs:** These basics help you get quality rest on the bus or in unfamiliar hotel rooms.
- **Travel Blanket:** A small, cozy blanket can make a huge difference on cold buses or add comfort to hotel rooms.
- **Sleep Aid Supplements:** Consider melatonin or magnesium if sleep is disrupted. Always consult with a medical professional before use.

4. Health and Hygiene

- **Portable First Aid Kit:** Include basics like band-aids, antiseptic wipes, pain relief medication, and blister care to handle minor injuries on the go.
- **Hand Sanitizer and Disinfectant Wipes:** To keep germs at bay, especially when constantly on the move and in communal environments.
- **Sunscreen and Lip Balm:** Protection against the sun, especially for outdoor games and travel.
- **Hydration Tablets for Replenishment:** For intensive recovery after long, hot days.

5. Mental Resilience and Entertainment

- **Noise-Canceling Headphones:** Vital for blocking out distractions on buses or in loud environments.
- **Portable Chargers and Charging Cables:** Ensures you're never without power for your devices.

- **Books, Podcasts, and Audiobooks:** Great for mental relaxation and personal development during downtime.
- **Journal or Notebook:** Writing can be a helpful outlet for stress relief and tracking goals, experiences, or workouts.
- **Mindfulness or Meditation Apps:** Guided meditation can be a valuable tool for managing stress and staying focused.

While the unpredictable and disruptive nature of the minor league experience can be disorienting, these easy preparations can significantly improve the experience, preparing you for whatever life on the road throws at you.

While the road through the minor leagues can be daunting, there are many positives to the experience. First, anyone who enters professional baseball becomes one of the best players in the world —it is a very exclusive club to have played professional baseball. Lifelong relationships are built, and the skills acquired, like resiliency and toughness, are enduring skills that will cross over into life after baseball. The pursuit of a dream and the hard work that it takes to obtain that dream will forever mold how an athlete lives their life, even though the challenge at the professional level is extreme. And for those that do make it to the major leagues, there is nothing like that lifestyle, and making their major league debut will make the entire road worth it.

CONCLUSION

At the heart of this book is a single, powerful message: There's a better way for athletes to reach the highest levels of baseball. This path prioritizes the athlete's genuine growth, ensuring families avoid being drawn into a profit-driven process and instead make informed decisions based on what truly benefits their child. Traditionally, this process has often been dominated by organizations seeking to profit from it, leaving unsuspecting and under-informed families and athletes at a disadvantage. This book aims to demonstrate that there is indeed a better way to reach the highest levels and navigate this journey.

I want to express my gratitude to all the readers who have taken the time and made the investment to support their athlete's dreams by purchasing and reading this book.

I understand that navigating this process can feel overwhelming, especially in an industry crowded with voices that don't always prioritize the best interests of young athletes. My goal with this book is to provide a clear roadmap that helps families avoid unnecessary stress while equipping them with the tools to make educated, confident decisions.

I sincerely hope that the strategies outlined in this book lead to a more seamless process, enabling more children to achieve their dreams. From this point forward, I envision a future filled with hope —one where families no longer experience anxiety or a lack of understanding about this process but instead guide their children toward levels of success they've never imagined before.

With these strategies, families can approach this journey with confidence and excitement, replacing confusion with clarity. Together, we can redefine the standard, allowing young athletes to surpass boundaries and fulfill dreams they may have once thought unattainable.

To every parent, coach, and young athlete, I encourage you to apply the lessons shared here, focus on authentic growth, and keep striving forward with the belief that this journey can be as enriching as it is successful. Here's to a future filled with new opportunities and milestones, where each step forward is meaningful and purposeful.

For those who want to learn more about navigating this process the right way and with more precision, we encourage you to reach out to us at KPI by submitting a form at kpimh.com. We have a host of options for both in-house and remote training that can serve athletes at every level, living anywhere in the country. We have changed player development in Northern California and are now ready to provide a better plan to aspiring athletes across the nation.

THANK YOU FOR READING MY BOOK!

DOWNLOAD YOUR FREE GIFT
Just to say thanks for buying and reading my book,
I would like to give you free access to a recruiting
webinar where I dive deep into navigating
the recruiting process.

I appreciate your interest in my book and value your feedback as it helps me improve future versions of this book. I would appreciate it if you could leave your invaluable review on Amazon.com with your feedback.

Thank you!

www.ingramcontent.com/pod-product-compliance
Lightning Source LLC
Chambersburg PA
CBHW030242010526
44107CB00030B/1306/J